G000150701

Enfield Libraries

RIDGE AVENUE LIBRARY			
RIDGE AVENUE WINCHMORE HILL LONDON N21 2RH TEL: 020 8360 9662			
✓ Cat 30/8/01 ew			

Please remember that this item will attract overdue charges if not returned by the latest date stamped above. You may renew it in person, by telephone or by post quoting the barcode number and your library card number.

ENFIELD
Leisure Services
working with you

30126 01531097 9

ENHANCING QUALITY IN ASSESSMENT

edited by Wynne Harlen

A publication of the BERA Policy
Task Group on Assessment

Paul Chapman
Publishing Ltd

Selection Copyright © British Educational Research Association
(BERA) 1994. All other material © as credited.

All rights reserved

Paul Chapman Publishing Ltd
144 Liverpool Road
London
N1 1LA

Apart from any fair dealing for the purposes of research or
private study, or criticism or review, as permitted under the
Copyright, Designs and Patents Acts, 1988, this publication may be
reproduced, stored or transmitted, in any form or by any means,
only with the prior permission in writing of the publishers, or
in the case of reprographic reproduction in accordance with the
terms of licences issued by the Copyright Licensing Agency.
Inquiries concerning reproduction outside those terms should be
sent to the publishers at the above mentioned address.

British Library Cataloguing in Publication Data

Enhancing Quality in Assessment
  I. Harlen, Wynne
  371.26

  ISBN 1-85396-260-0

Typeset by Dorwyn Ltd, Rowlands Castle, Hants
Printed and bound by Athenaeum Press, Newcastle upon Tyne

A b C D E F G H   9 8 7 6 5 4

CONTENTS

DEDICATION

This book is dedicated to the memory of Desmond Nuttall, our colleague, our friend and often our inspiration. Desmond was a member of the British Educational Association's Task Group on Assessment, which produced this book, from the time of the group's inception in 1989 until his death in October 1993. Although assessment was only one of the fields in which he made a lasting contribution, it was the main thread running through his brilliant career in educational research and the one in which he made important contributions to policy issues. The many references to his work in the chapters of this book give an indication of the extent of this contribution. We value his work and miss him greatly.

CONTRIBUTORS

Harry Black is the Deputy Director of the Scottish Council for Research in Education. He has written widely on assessment which supports good teaching and learning. He has a wide range of research experience spanning primary through to tertiary education.

Patricia Broadfoot is Professor of Education and Head of the School of Education at Bristol University. She has researched extensively into assessment policy and practice and is currently jointly directing a national study of the impact of the National Curriculum and its assessment at Key Stage 2. As editor of *Comparative Education* and joint editor of *Assessment in Education*, her contribution to this volume represents her strong interest in and commitment to studying developments in assessment in an international perspective.

Richard Daugherty is Professor of Education and Head of the Department of Education at the University of Wales, Aberystwyth. Among his research interests are national assessment policy and assessment procedures in public examinations. He has been a member of the School Examinations and Assessment Council and from 1991 to 1993, he chaired the Curriculum Council for Wales. His publications include *GCSE in Wales*, Welsh Office, 1991.

Caroline Gipps is a Reader in Education at the University of London Institute of Education. A primary teacher, psychologist and researcher by training, she has carried out a wide range of research on the uses and impact of assessment; she has published widely both in this area and in the critical evaluation of assessment developments. She was President of BERA in 1992–93, and is Executive Editor of *Assessment in Education*.

Wynne Harlen has been Director of the Scottish Council for Research in Education since 1990 and was previously Professor of Science Education at the University of Liverpool. She began her professional life as a teacher and college lecturer in science and since 1965 has been engaged in curriculum research, development and assessment. She has published 18 books and contributed to 25 others. She has worked for regular short periods in developing countries and produced four publications for UNESCO. She was awarded the OBE for services to education in 1991.

Mary James is a Lecturer at the University of Cambridge Institute of Education where she teaches on in-service teacher education courses. Her special interests are in the area of curriculum, assessment and evaluation. She is the editor of *The Curriculum Journal* and has co-authored a major text on *Curriculum Evaluation in Schools*. Her current research is on the practice of moderation in National Curriculum Assessment at Key Stage One. Previously she was involved in the national evaluation of pilot records of achievement schemes in secondary schools, with Patricia Broadfoot. Before she took up her post at Cambridge, she worked at the Open University. And before that, she taught for ten years in secondary schools.

David Satterly was formerly Senior Lecturer in Education at the University of Bristol. He has recently been carrying out research in the Autonomous University of Yucàtan, Mexico.

ACRONYMS AND ABBREVIATIONS

AERA	American Educational Research Association
AIAA	Association of Inspectors and Advisers for Assessment
ASAT	Australian Scholastic Aptitude Test
AT	attainment target
BERA	British Educational Research Association
CSE	Certificate of Secondary Education
DES	Department of Education and Science
DfE	Department for Education
FE	further education
GCE	General Certificate of Education
GCSE	General Certificate of Secondary Education
GEST	grants for education support and training
HMI	Her Majesty's Inspector
HSC	Higher School Certificate
ILEA	Inner London Education Authority
JMB	Joint Matriculation Board
KMK	*Kultusminister Konferenz*
KS1	Key Stage 1
LEA	local education authority
LMS	local management of schools
NCA	National Curriculum assessment
NCVQ	National Council for Vocational Qualifications
NISEAC	Northern Ireland Schools Examination and Assessment Council
NVQ	National Vocational Qualifications

NZQA	New Zealand Qualifications Authority
OFSTED	Office for Standards in Education
PES	public examination subject
PSD	personal and social development
SAR	student achievement record
SAS	school-assessed subject
SAT	standard assessment test/task
SCAA	School Curriculum and Assessment Authority
SCOTVEC	Scottish Vocational Education Council
SEAC	School Examination and Assessment Council
SEB	Scottish Examination Board
SEC	Secondary Examinations Council
SED	Scottish Education Department
SOED	Scottish Office Education Department
SSABSA	Senior Secondary Assessment Board of South Australia
ST	standard task/test (also known as SAT)
TA	teacher assessment
TE	tertiary entrance
TER	tertiary entrance rank
TES	tertiary entrance score
TGAT	Task Group on Assessment and Testing
UBMT	unbiased mean total
YTS	Youth Training Scheme

INTRODUCTION

Wynne Harlen

The authors of this book, members of the British Educational Research Association's Policy Task Group on Assessment, have been concerned at the accelerating move to return to formal procedures in national tests and examinations. A major issue has been the quite explicit downgrading over recent years of assessments made by teachers. Although one of the worst examples of this, in the procedures for producing national test results, has been reversed by the Dearing recommendations (Dearing, 1994), there is a good way to go before we achieve the kind of confidence in teachers' assessment that is found, for example, in Germany. At the same time we recognise that teachers' assessments are sometimes more unreliable than would be the case if more resources were used to research the reasons and support measures to improve procedures. There are particular problems in criterion-referenced assessment, for example, which are common to teachers' assessment and to examination boards. Collectively the chapters of this book examine the issues concerning what is meant by quality in assessment and the procedures used, in this country and abroad, for improving assessment through moderation, both of the process and of the results, procedures which are now described as relating to quality assurance and quality control.

Assessment is the process of making judgements about a student's performance in a particular task. The result will clearly depend upon what the task is and how the judgement is made, in relation to what standards or criteria. It will also depend upon other factors which affect

Copyright © 1994, Wynne Harlen

performance, such as the student's motivation, perception of the relevance of the task and anxiety about the consequences of success or failure. The influence of these affective factors must not be forgotten whilst we focus on the task and on how performance in it is judged; neither are the personal factors independent of the formal ones. However, the main concern in this book is with those aspects of assessment which are intended to be part of the process.

As educational researchers, we have based our discussion on evidence from research without, we hope, making references to sources too obtrusive. We are well aware that policies and practices are determined by many factors, with research evidence often being given much less than top priority. Nevertheless it is important to bring together what is known in order to present our position rigorously and to inform others who seek evidence on which to base their ideas and practices. We believe that the arguments and evidence presented here, although for the most part based in the educational experience and systems of the UK will inform debate about assessment beyond this country. For wherever problems in assessment practice are faced, and particularly where changes are towards broadening beyond traditional forms of tests and examinations, to encompassing skills and knowledge application rather than knowledge recall and to criterion-referencing, then the issues discussed here will arise.

Internal and external assessment

It is convenient to make a simple distinction between 'internal' and 'external' assessment procedures, whilst recognising the danger of oversimplification. The distinction involves not only who makes the judgements but who sets the tasks. Thus there are theoretically four combinations of internally or externally set tasks which are internally or externally marked. Given that the chief rationale for internal assessment is in terms of validity, to allow what is assessed to be more like 'real life', then the important distinction is between internally and externally set tasks. Therefore the term 'internal assessment' is used to describe assessment where the task is part of the normal teaching and learning or is determined by the teachers to suit the context and content of learning, usually within the guidelines of an externally defined framework. Assessment of an externally set task, even though the response may be marked and judged by the teacher, is regarded as being 'external'.

The description of quality in these two aspects – task and process of judgement – educes respectively the two concepts of validity and reliability. As discussed in Chapter 1, validity refers to how well the task that is presented to a student when an assessment is made 'reflects the skill, knowledge, attitude or other quality it was intended to assess' while reliability 'refers to the extent to which a similar result would be obtained if the assessment were to be repeated' (p. 12). Reliability and validity are not independent concepts; in combination they contribute to an overarching notion of 'dependability' in assessment, that is, just how far a result can be relied upon as being a useful and fair statement of a student's achievement. Reliability and validity are often in tension, for to increase the former it is necessary to standardise the task possibly to the point where it infringes validity. This is a point echoed in several places in this book since it underlies the concern for addressing ways of improving reliability without endangering validity.

All forms of assessment, whether internal or external, are subject to human judgement and thus require some form of moderation. The need may perhaps seem minimal where external, machine-marked tests or examinations are concerned, but in these the selection of items and the creation of marking schemes, crucial to the outcome, are based on judgements which will vary from one test constructor to another. It is because the focus of attention has in the past been on the marking and judging to the neglect of the task setting that the assumption has been allowed to persist for long that external tests and examinations are dependable whilst internal assessment is not. Furthermore, as Chapter 3 shows, the notion that the marking of external tests and examination is of high reliability should be challenged. Indeed Chapter 3 provides evidence and arguments to suggest that the reliability of external assessment is not so great as to compensate for its shortcomings in terms of validity. Which brings us back to the importance of validity and to the nature of the task that is undertaken when assessment is carried out.

There are two central pillars to the argument that for a number of outcomes of education, internal assessment is essential for worthwhile evidence of achievement. One of these concerns the influence of context on performance. It is well established that 'assessment (like learning) is highly context-specific and one generalises at one's peril' (Nuttall, 1987, p. 115). Tests, whether internally or externally set, can provide only a limited number of tasks and thus a small sample of possible ones involving a particular skill or ability from which to generalise. Moreover, the interaction of personal factors such as motivation with particular contexts means that providing the same tasks for all is not necessarily providing equal opportunity. For example, boys and girls respond differently to tasks set in contexts which have a conventional gender identity. On the other hand, internal assessment which can gather evidence from performance in a wide range of tasks, indeed as wide as the range in which teaching and learning takes place, provides a much larger sample of performance and thus a more valid basis for judging a student's achievement.

The second point about the validity of internal assessment relates to the recognition that central to the aims of education is the development of mental and physical skills, values, attitudes and applicable knowledge and understanding as well as mastery of a traditional and enduring body of knowledge. National curricula and examination syllabuses (see p. 14, for example) make such objectives explicit. Assessment for whatever purpose must reflect this broad range of aims and must, therefore, provide opportunities for students to show these skills, attitudes and abilities. Not only is this in many cases logistically impossible within the constraints of an externally set task but often it is logically impossible to do this, for example to assess by such means the ability to work co-operatively, or to apply knowledge in tackling unexpected problems in a study or project. It is only in a school-based assessment that appropriate and valid tasks can be provided for abilities such as these.

These arguments were readily accepted by the architects of the General Certificate of Secondary Education (GCSE) (see Chapter 6, p. 101) and of the Scottish National Certificate (Chapter 5). However, as set out in Chapter 6 in relation to the GCSE, 'Policy-makers have come to their own conclusions about coursework and its moderation, finding both to be, to an extent, unsatisfactory' (p. 109). There has been a distinct shift back to preference for external assessment in England, Wales and Northern Ireland, a shift which ignores both the deficiencies of this type of assessment and the possibilities and benefits of improving the quality of internal assessment.

The comparative dimension

It is the intention of this book to take a positive approach to improving the dependability of assessment carried out by teachers. One contribution to this is a review of possible practices in the UK and in other countries. The differences in the practices and in attempts to improve quality in assessment in six countries reviewed in Chapter 2 are particularly striking. But in the face of the available alternatives, policy-makers and practitioners, parents and pupils, cling tenaciously to their own views about how things should be conducted. These views, variously compounded of prejudice, habit and experience, are so pervasive that alternatives can seem almost literally impossible. One somewhat ironic consequence of this is that the very practices which have acquired an unassailable legitimacy in one cultural context are the same ones that are unthinkable in another.

But while such differences in educational assumptions and the policies and practices to which they give rise may be lamentable from a strictly empiricist point of view, they are in no sense arbitrary. Rather they are rooted in institutional and cultural traditions which are as complex in their various historical origins as they are difficult to change. Recent experience in Britain provides graphic testimony to the way in which politicians can cling to assumptions about education which reflect new, and indeed antithetical, ideologies. Thus, we have noted the return to external examination despite the recognition of the importance of curriculum goals which cannot be adequately assessed by them and the evidence of their inhibiting effect on many students. Similarly, in Australia, student achievements across a number of subjects are often reduced to a tertiary entrance score (Chapter 2, p. 41) in order to facilitate a rank-order decision-making despite widespread criticism of this practice.

In short, decisions concerning education are always heavily overlaid by assumptions rooted in cultural traditions. No amounts of evidence concerning technical quality of any particular form of educational assessment in terms of validity and reliability will be sufficient to render credible procedures which run counter to the dogmas of tradition. By the same token, procedures which are technically flawed or unsuitable for the purpose for which they are being used are unlikely to succumb to technical critiques if they enjoy the political and/or public credibility of familiarity and tradition.

This study of assessment quality cannot, therefore, be only a technical one. It must also be concerned with the social context of assessment, with what James and Conner (1993) refers to as its *credibility*. This theme runs throughout the book. Satterly's review of the quality of external assessment represents one of the ways in which we seek to challenge those orthodoxies of traditions which are not helpful in promoting greater quality in assessment as defined by today's educational priorities. Another is to attack the myths which may prevent possible alternatives from even appearing credible through employing a comparative perspective and juxtaposing against practices in the UK described in Chapters 5, 6 and 7 the very different ones which are currently in use in the education systems of a number of otherwise broadly comparable advanced nations.

Trends in moderation practice

Whilst Chapter 1 attempts to provide a view of quality in assessment and a framework for considering the pros and cons of various approaches to quality assurance and quality control described in the rest of the book, the nature of moderation is another of the themes which thread across all chapters. In some countries moderation is not regarded as a particularly relevant concept and so not defined except implicitly in practice. In other cases the definition implies a particular view of assessment and of the relative importance of quality control and quality assurance. The former is implied by definitions which are couched in terms of adjusting assessment results and the latter in terms of ensuring that the process of arriving at the results in sound. Some of the definitions cited in Chapter 6 – for example, moderation as 'the process of aligning standards in internal assessment' (p. 104) – hint at both and indicate that there is not always a clear distinction in practice.

However, the quality control/assurance description does help in elucidating a further theme which runs through the range of practices described in this book. This concerns the weight of decisions and consequences for the pupils or teachers which hangs on the assessment, that is, how high are the stakes. Perhaps not surprisingly quality control is likely to be perceived as paramount when stakes are high. By the same token, quality assurance, with its concern for professional development and feedback, may seem to have priority only when the stakes are low. Since the stakes in terms of the consequences for the student tend to be higher the older the student, there is also a pattern of greater concern for quality control in the upper secondary school and for quality control at lower school levels.

It follows from these trends that when stakes are high for teachers and schools, that is, when results are used for league tables, we can expect concern to drift to quality control even in the primary school. This would detract from the value of moderation procedures for the professional development of teachers and, in our view, the quality of moderation (p. 24) would suffer. That attention to quality assurance will reduce the problems of quality control in the long run is a claim endorsed by the arguments and evidence in this book.

Structure of the book

The chapters fall into two kinds. The first four are concerned with the range of practices in student assessment and with the steps taken in each to enhance quality, that is, in our terms, to provide 'information of the highest validity and optimum reliability suited to a particular purpose and context'. The following three chapters describe studies of the quality of teacher-based assessment in three different contexts: further education (FE) in Scotland, the General Certificate of Secondary Education

(GCSE) in England and Wales and the National Curriculum assessment
at the end of Key Stage 1 (age seven years) in England.

Chapter 1. Issues and Approaches to Quality Assurance and Quality Control in Assessment

Wynne Harlen takes as a starting point the desirable quality of any
assessment, that it should be dependable. This concept of dependability
combines validity and reliability, which are competing requirements.
The extent to which priority should be given to one or the other depends
on the purpose and the context of a particular assessment. The argument
leads to the proposal that 'quality in assessment is the provision of
information of the highest validity and optimum reliability suited to a
particular purpose and context'. Arguments in favour of teacher assessment as compared with external assessment for various purposes are set
out briefly, as a precursor to extension in later chapters. At the same
time it is recognised that there is a need to enhance the comparability, a
particular form of reliability, of teacher assessment through moderation.
Various approaches to moderation as quality control and as quality
assurance are outlined and the chapter concludes with a discussion of
quality in moderation.

Chapter 2. Approaches to Quality Assurance and Control in Six Countries

In this chapter Patricia Broadfoot exemplifies approaches to quality
assurance and control in countries outside the UK, taking six countries
comparable to the UK in their educational traditions and aspirations:
the USA, Germany, Sweden, France, New Zealand and Australia.
However, Broadfoot does more than show different ways of achieving
similar aims; she considers the social and historical contexts which have
lead to different approaches. Whilst recognising that practices cannot
simply be transplanted from one culture to another, the comparative
component 'not only helps to illuminate complex relationships of cause
and effect but it can also stimulate the questioning of existing practice'.

Chapter 3. Quality in External Assessment

David Satterly takes as a starting point for his critical look at external
assessment, the ideal requirements, of generalisability, validity and reliability of assessment for certain purposes. He then examines the problems posed in realising these ideals in practice. Satterly draws on a wide

range of research studies in a critical review which challenges the prevailing assumption in the UK that external assessment and examinations are more dependable and valid than internal assessment: research evidence which shows, for example, that external examinations that are marked by several assessors are no more reliable than teachers' estimates. Satterly notes that 'given the requirement to publish exam results by which schools can be compared', it is time for this 'to be matched by similar openness about reliability of the great body of external assessment on which these comparisons rest.'

Chapter 4. Quality in Teacher Assessment

Caroline Gipps describes the characteristics, contexts and purposes of assessment by teachers. She clarifies the notion of formative assessment and distinguishes it from other purposes of teacher assessment. Drawing on her research into assessment practice by infants' teachers, Gipps describes these teachers' assessment practices, identifying three 'models'. She then turns to the process of group moderation as a means of enhancing the quality of teachers' assessments through developing a consensus about the meaning of criteria and using them as a basis for judgements. The proposals on moderation put forward in the report of the Task Group on Assessment and Testing (TGAT) are examined critically and in relation to the later developments in moderation designed to ensure consistency across teachers both in approach and judgements. Gipps warns against a return to the TGAT-style statistical moderation, hinted at in the Dearing Report, 'since consistency of standards is not the prime requirement if the cost is to validity and teachers' professional involvement'.

Chapter 5. The Quality of Assessment in Further Education in Scotland

Harry Black describes research on the new assessment procedures brought into further education colleges in Scotland by the introduction of a modular structure for courses leading to vocational qualifications at various levels. The changes were far-reaching, including the specification of criterion-referenced assessment as part of module descriptors and assessment that was essentially skill based and lecturer based. Black describes staff responses to the changes as having three stages. The first or initial stage was of coming to terms with the meaning of the changes and grasping the new format and language of module description. In the second stage professional challenges were met, including realising the practical problems of comparability in applying criteria. The third stage was reached when staff felt comfortable and confident with the new system and were operating internal quality assurance systems and reflecting on the role of external course assessors. In summary, Black concludes that the difficulties encountered 'can be ameliorated particularly by strategies which encourage staff to share their understandings and their difficulties'.

Chapter 6. Quality Assurance, Teacher Assessments and Public Examinations

Richard Daugherty focuses in this chapter on the coursework assessment component of public examinations at the age of sixteen. Research into the operation of coursework moderation systems reveals that teachers express a need for greater emphasis on quality assurance, whilst examining bodies strive for quality control. Daugherty notes that the reliability of teachers' assessment of coursework has been called into question, more by politicians than by Her Majesty's Inspectors (HMI) and those involved in its operation. Indeed he expresses surprise that there have not been more problems, given the extent of the innovation and relative lack of experience in this aspect of external examination. He also points out that problems of comparability in formal examinations are not exposed to the same outside scrutiny as are the assessments of coursework carried out by teachers. He suggests that, rather than to reduce the element of coursework, 'More might be achieved, without undue restrictions on teachers in setting and marking their students' work, by clarifying the rules governing the setting of tasks, how they are marked and the selection of work for moderation.'

Chapter 7. Experience of Quality Assurance at Key Stage 1

In this chapter Mary James reports studies of moderation of Key Stage 1 National Curriculum assessment in six East Anglian local education authorities (LEAs) between 1990 and 1993. The research examines how the LEAs met the obligations placed on them to set up arrangements to moderate teachers' assessments and the administration and marking of the standard tests (STs), an entirely new and to some extent alien activity in infants schools. James notes that 'the attempt to introduce new systems is equivalent to bringing about cultural change and must, therefore, be framed according to a timescale and with attention to the human dimensions that cultural change entails'. The chapter also explores the proposals for moderation in the Dearing Report and the implications of these for some resolution of the tension between quality assurance and quality control in the future.

Note

I am grateful to Particia Broadfoot for some of the material included in this introduction.

References

Dearing, Sir R. (1994) *The National Curriculum and its Assessment: Final Report*, School Curriculum and Assessment Authority (SCAA), London.

James, M. and Conner, C. (1993) Are reliability and validity achievable in National Curriculum assessment? Some observations on moderation at Key Stage 1 in 1992, *The Curriculum Journal*, Vol. 4, no. 1, pp. 5–19.

Nuttall, D. L. (1987) The validity of assessment, *European Journal of Psychology of Education*, Vol. II, pp. 109–18.

1
ISSUES AND APPROACHES TO QUALITY ASSURANCE AND QUALITY CONTROL IN ASSESSMENT

Wynne Harlen

The concept of quality in assessment

Assessment takes place in a wide range of contexts in education and for many different purposes. Purposes relating to individual pupils include informing the next steps in teaching, summarising achievement at a certain time, selection, certification and guidance. These all affect a pupil's immediate or longer-term opportunities and call for as much fairness and accuracy in the assessment as is possible. Pupils are also assessed for other purposes, such as surveys of national achievement and for research, where the results will not have a direct effect on the pupils assessed but, none the less, a dependable result is required. Such statements beg questions about what we mean by 'accuracy' and 'dependability' in this context and to what degree we can expect to achieve these qualities in educational assessment.

A comprehensive definition of assessment includes the processes of gathering, interpreting, recording and use of information about a pupil's response to an educational task (Harlen *et al.*, 1992, p. 217). A vast range of ways of assessing can be identified by combining different means of getting information (e.g. observing actions, listening, reading written work, studying products such as drawings and artefacts) with various kinds of task (e.g. written test or examination papers, practical tasks set externally or by the teacher, projects, tasks undertaken as part of normal class work). In the case of formal assessments there are

Copyright © 1994, Wynne Harlen

further variations introduced by whether the marking is carried out by an external agency or by the teacher and the reference base used for interpretation (norm-referenced, criterion-referenced or pupil-referenced).

The reason for choosing one rather than another of this plethora of possible ways of assessing relates to the requirement for optimum dependability. This word needs to be understood in terms of the two interconnected concepts of reliability and validity since its meaning is otherwise ambiguous. The problem can be illustrated by asking the question: is a written science test more or less dependable than a practical science test? If dependable is taken to mean that the result would be similar if the test were repeated, then the written test would come out best. But if it means the one that is the most dependable measure of how practical science tasks are tackled, then the reverse could be the case. So these two aspects have to be disentangled.

The concept of *reliability* of the result of an assessment refers to the extent to which a similar result would be obtained if the assessment were to be repeated. The aspect of an assessment which refers to how well the result really reflects the skill, knowledge, attitude or other quality it was intended to assess is described as its *validity*. These are two distinct attributes of an assessment, as the example of the science test suggests, but they are also interconnected. An assessment which is low in reliability, that is, gives widely varying results if repeated, can hardly have a high validity, since it will be unclear just what is being assessed. Conversely it is difficult in some cases to have high reliability *and* high validity, since the requirements of high reliability lead to close specification of task, response mode, means of gathering information and interpretation and these are often incompatible with high validity. For example, a standardised reading test has high reliability when children are required to read isolated words, free of context. The results, however, are a less valid assessment of how well children can read when using context to help them, an ability which would be tested by a more realistic (but less reliable) reading task.

The highly significant, and sometimes overlooked, consequence of this argument that validity and reliability can never both be 100 per cent, is that we must recognise assessment is never 'accurate' in the way that the word is used in the context of measurement in the physical world. Assessment in education is inherently inexact and it should be treated as such. We should not expect to be able to measure pupils' abilities with the same confidence as we can measure their heights. This in no way makes educational assessment useless. It means that the interpretation of assessment results should be in terms of being an indication of what pupils can do but not an exact specification. At the same time this is no excuse for failing to make every effort to ensure that both validity and reliability are at an optimum level, for information which is low in these qualities cannot be used effectively and, if used, could lead to injustice.

Both reliability and validity have to be considered in relation to the *contexts* and *purposes* of assessment. A highly reliable assessment but one which is time consuming or demanding of resources will be of little use to a teacher who wants information about pupils on a regular basis with minimum interruption of normal work. In such circumstances *quality* in assessment means an assessment made and interpreted on the spot which provides the type of information required (high validity) and with the greatest degree of reliability possible in the circumstances. The intended use of the information in this case means that reliability is not the foremost consideration. However, had the purpose been to provide an assessment of coursework as a contribution to an external award, the burden on reliability could be greater. In both cases, however, the value depends on the ability of the teacher to gather and interpret the information with the required rigour and respect for evidence. Good assessment thus depends on the use and development of these skills. These sorts of consideration lead to the proposition that *quality in assessment is the provision of information of the highest validity and optimum reliability suited to a particular purpose and context.*

Why teacher assessment?

The usefulness of an assessment is directly related to its validity, providing it is not so low in reliability as to call this into question. This is saying no more than that if we want information about, say, a student's ability to solve mathematical problems, we need to have assessed them trying to solve mathematical problems. Results of a reliably marked arithmetic test will not be useful for this purpose. Thus as a priority for ensuring quality in assessment, validity has first consideration. Thereafter every effort has to be made to increase reliability and in this pursuit tightness of specification of task and interpretation adopted is the highest that is still compatible with required validity.

It is not difficult to see that, for the purpose of assessing many attributes, formal tests and examinations do not compare very favourably with less restricted methods of assessment. This is well demonstrated by the list of skills and abilities identified by the Secondary Examinations Council (SEC) as needing to be assessed through coursework in the GCSE:

(a) the ability to use and develop techniques for making and recording accurate observations, in the context of, for example, fieldwork or experimental work;

(b) research skills, including the ability to organise the systematic collection and ordering of pertinent information; familiarity with and use of a wide range of sources; the ability to distinguish sources of different status in weighing evidence – for example, primary and secondary sources;

(c) interactive skills (responding appropriately to the consequences of an earlier action); such interaction may be with people, information sources (including information technology), tools or concrete materials;

(d) the ability to find a role and co-operate with others in an activity;

(e) motor skills including manipulation of apparatus, operation of machinery, and marking out and processing of materials;

(f) skills involving a sense of timing; the ability to 'think on one's feet';

(g) the exercise of safety awareness;

(h) the ability to design, conduct and evaluate a simple experiment or survey to test some hypothesis or illuminate some issue;

(i) the ability to make a simple theoretical model of a 'real-life' situation and to test and refine the model by examining both it and the real-life situation further;

(j) the determination and ability to sustain a chosen study from conception to realisation;

(k) attainment in tasks which, by their nature, require time for exploration; investigational, planning and design activities where several approaches may need to be considered before a specific solution is developed; activities where several resource constraints (such as those of cost, time and skill) have to be investigated and weighed before a solution is pursued;

(l) attainment in areas where it is desirable to allow time for reflection, for example, in articulating a thoughtful personal response to the expressive arts or to religious experience or in teaching an objective and informed view of some current social or moral issue;

(m) skills of adaptation and improvisation in the widest sense: the ability to restructure information or modify objects to suit immediate needs; the ability periodically to review the progress of a long-term enterprise (such as a scientific experiment, a piece of planning or a craft or agricultural project) and to change tactics if necessary; the exercise of awareness of possible sources of difficulty or error.

(SEC, 1985)

Other items could be added to the list which are equally important objectives of education and ones most valued in the modern world, as indicated by their inclusion in concepts such as 'enterprise', higher-order thinking abilities and transferable skills. Unless the assessment includes these attributes they will be undervalued and underdeveloped.

The key feature relating to the validity of assessment of any kind, but which is particularly relevant to our present argument, is that of *opportunity* for the students to show that they have the abilities, skills, etc. in question. So, for each of the items in the above list, we should ask 'What conditions/situations give students opportunity to show the ability or skill?' It is not difficult to realise that most require assessment to be made over an extended time and in conditions which approach 'realistic' situations; many cannot validly be assessed in short periods of time under examination conditions and none can be validly assessed by written items alone. Since situations which provide opportunity for these abilities to be used and developed must exist in teaching, then it follows that coursework can also provide opportunity for valid assessment.

Similar points apply to the assessment of young children, where the notion of opportunity is equally useful. At the simplest level, a child may be able to draw and discuss his or her ideas with the teacher but not to write them down. Thus a written task would not provide opportunity for the ideas to be assessed whilst the normal classroom activities would do so. The point is wider, however, than just avoiding the use of skills (such as reading and writing) which are not under test. It extends to the meaning children perceive for a task, their past experience of it, their interest in it. It is well established that these things influence performance. Thus giving the same task to children under the same conditions is not necessarily providing equal opportunity for them to show what they can do or what they know. A more valid assessment would be made across a range of situations, such as can be done by a teacher assessing as an ongoing part of teaching.

However, the matter of reliability must be faced, for, as stated earlier, an unreliable assessment is not only of little use but can be unjust. The endeavour to increase reliability is common to all methods of assessment but the context and purpose of assessment will affect the degree of priority given to reliability. A higher priority is necessarily accorded to it when the measurement of attainment contributes to the certification of the student or, in aggregated form, to an evaluation of the performance of teachers and schools. Where a teacher is assessing his/her pupils in order to feed back into helping their learning, reliability need not be a major consideration.

It is recognised that constant attention has to be given to the reliability of external examinations with papers being re-marked and results adjusted. In these circumstances the tasks to which students respond are pre-specified and the conditions under which students respond are controlled. Procedures are required both to monitor consistency of presentation of the tasks in practice and to standardise marking but the inherent uniformity of tasks and conditions in examinations suggests dependability. However, as Chapter 3 indicates, the higher reliability of examinations over teacher-based assessment should not be taken for granted (for example, see p. 62).

Nevertheless, traditionally there has been more confidence in external examinations in the UK and less in coursework or teacher assessment. The key role of the latter, which we have argued in terms of validity and opportunity, indicates that it is important to increase confidence in this area. The means of achieving this is through various procedures which until recently were described as various forms of moderation. The varieties of moderation are about as extensive as the variety of methods of assessment and the rest of this chapter attempts to review the range and to suggest a framework for describing and comparing different approaches.

Moderation: quality assurance and quality control

Moderation procedures have been devised in order to reduce those sources of error which are seen to be greatest in particular circumstances whilst at the same time preserving validity of assessment as required for quality in assessment. The sources of error include variation in the demand or opportunity provided by the tasks undertaken by students, differences in interpretation of performance criteria or marking schemes and the intrusion of irrelevant contextual information in making judgements (as illustrated in Chapter 5, p. 92). Categorising the variety of measures taken to reduce such errors risks the oversimplification of any classification system, and the usual caveats apply here. Against these disadvantages have to be placed the advantage that categorisation provides a basis for comparing the pros and cons of various methods.

At an initial level of categorisation, moderation procedures fall fairly readily into one of two kinds:

(i)   those concerned essentially with adjustment of the outcome of assessment to improve fairness for groups and individuals;
(ii) those concerned with the process of arriving at fair assessments for groups and individuals, which will, in some cases, extend to opportunities to learn as well as to be assessed.

The first of these takes place after the assessment has been made and is designed to ensure fairness by adjusting results where there seems to be inconsistency or systematic differences in the way procedures have been followed. For example, there may be a 'reference test' given to all students against which coursework or teacher assessments are compared. The marking of the latter may be adjusted to put students from one teacher in the same rank order as given by the reference test. Moderation of this kind is also called into play when two forms of assessment are combined, as for example in the National Curriculum assessment, when teacher assessment and standard task results are combined. According to the procedures used in 1991 and 1992, teachers could request moderation if they considered that accepting the standard task result would be unfair.

Types of moderation of the second kind take place *before* the assessment is completed. They are designed to improve the process of assessment in order to 'ensure that consistency has been achieved, rather than to impose it on an otherwise inconsistent assessment system' (NISEAC, 1991, para. 10.1). The quotation is from a document which proposed moderation procedures for the national assessment in Northern Ireland which illustrate well this formative approach. The kinds of action proposed involved teachers meeting to discuss pupils' work both within one school and with teachers from other schools. Visits of moderators to schools were also proposed so that any systematic variation between teachers would be spotted. The overall purpose was, however, not to adjust marks and settle disputes, but to improve the quality of the assessment process.

The distinction between (i) and (ii) can be recognised as the distinction between quality control and quality assurance (e.g. Wiliam, 1992). In the industrial model, quality control is the process of weeding out the imperfect products, meaning those which fall outside certain tolerance limits. Quality assurance constantly monitors the steps in arriving at the product and, in making sure that all processes are optimally carried out, theoretically prevents imperfect products. This analogy might suggest that the distinction might be better described as concern with product or with process. Although useful, in the assessment context there is more interaction between impact on process and product. Not only is attention to improving the assessment process justified in terms of a more reliable product but the discussion of a possible change to an assessment outcome during the moderation process can have an impact on the process of arriving at future decisions. The role of moderators at Key Stage 1, described in Chapter 7 (p. 126) illustrates this interaction and the dilemma for the moderator of having a dual role in relation to both teachers' assessments and standard task administration.

The distinction between a quality assurance procedure and a quality control procedure does not reside inherently in the nature of the procedure; the categorisation must be made in terms of the purpose and effects of the procedure. To take an example well illustrated in later chapters, the meeting of teachers in groups to discuss students' work may have a quality control purpose if the result is that the judgements made about the work discussed are being scrutinised, or it may have a quality assurance purpose if examples of students' work are discussed in order to clarify the meaning of criteria but with no impact on the assessment of the particular examples. Thus group moderation appears under both quality assurance and quality control in the following accounts. Of course in some cases the procedures will have a dual function, since when teachers discuss specific cases it will almost inevitably have an impact on their own understanding of the criteria, but an essentially quality assurance process will not have a direct quality control function. Similarly almost all quality control procedures can have a quality assurance function if the results are fed back to pin-point the source of error and to help in removing it.

Moderation procedures of quality assurance or quality control are used to improve the essentially imperfect process of assessment, but themselves vary in efficiency and in other important features such as cost. Thus not all approaches to moderation are equally useful and viable and it is necessary to identify the features of quality in moderation, just as we have for quality in assessment. We shall consider this after first providing some brief accounts of the main approaches, taken under the headings of quality control and quality assurance.

Approaches to quality control in assessment

The common feature shared by procedures in this category is that they occur after the event. They vary, however, in other respects, which emerge from the following examples.

Use of reference or scaling tests for statistical moderation

This is a device for adjusting students' marks using results of an externally marked test taken by all students. It is used in some cases to adjust assessments made by teachers in order to compensate for systematic variations in teachers' judgements. The Australian Scholastic Aptitude Test (see p. 40) provides an example; others are described in Newbould and Massey (1979). In these cases the rank order of students assessed by one teacher or school stays the same but all scores may be moved up or down.

It is also used where comparisons have to be made between students who have been examined, either by internal or external assessment, in different subjects of which some may be easier than others, as in the calculation of the tertiary education rank in New South Wales (see p. 43). In this case the rank order of students is likely to be changed. In these and other variants on the procedure, the student, teacher and institution have no control of what happens. It happens automatically and without any participation of the teacher beyond supplying the raw scores.

Inspection of samples by post

Here work assessed internally by teachers for an external award is sampled by the examination centre, usually the awarding body, to check that tasks have been set as required and that they have been marked and graded according to instructions (see, for example, the account of the Joint Matriculation Board's procedures by Smith, 1978). Precise instructions for selecting samples are normally given, so the teacher does not exercise choice in the matter. Inspection of samples is the principal method currently used by examination boards for moderation of coursework assessment (see Chapter 6, p. 104). The procedure applies where written or other products on paper are used in assessment; thus where it is the only form of moderation there is a tendency for the assessment to be restricted to such forms.

Inspection of samples by visiting moderators

In principle this is similar to inspection by post but in practice the face-to-face contact between teacher and moderator or verifier facilitates professional discussion with reference to processes as well as to products. A wider range of products can be included in the assessment and moderation, although since the visit takes place after the work has been produced it cannot include ephemeral products or processes of working. The visiting moderation procedures of the Scottish Examination Board and several other similar boards illustrate this approach. The cost of such exercises is a considerable deterrent to their use except for a sample of institutions at any one time. However, this is the normal procedure for vocational qualifications such as those given by SCOTVEC and the NCVQ.

External examining

This is a further variation of moderation by inspection of samples. It is widespread practice in higher education, developed to prevent variation in standards of awards between institutions which grant their own degrees, diplomas, certificates, etc. Examinations in these institutions are internally set and internally marked and so are as much in need of moderation as are continuously assessed components which are clearly more dependent on the judgement of individual lecturers. Examiners sometimes comment on papers or tasks set and on procedures, but their chief function is to comment on the standard of work of the students who pass or are given various grades and in some cases this results in the adjustment of grades.

Teacher-requested moderation (appeals)

It is a feature of almost every certification procedure that an appeal can be made when the outcome is not what was expected. The appeal is usually on the grounds that the examination has not been carried out correctly and, when marking is at fault, the result can be changed. However, up to 1993 the national assessment arrangements allowed appeals on grounds other than that the assessment was faulty. Because the result of teachers' assessment and the result of the standard test or task had to be combined, with the latter taking precedence, there was the possibility that differences would arise due to the nature of the two types of information. One of the tasks of local education authority (LEA) moderators was to consider such appeals, although the process was initiated by the teacher (see Chapter 7, p. 121).

Group/consensus moderation of internal assessment

This involves the review of work which has been internally examined either as part or as the whole of an examination. The focus is the extent of agreement with the grade or scale point assigned to particular pieces of work by teachers. As already mentioned (p. 18) the process is little different from group moderation for quality assurance purposes, but the intention here is to ensure that grades have been assigned as agreed rather than to affect the process of arriving at the grading in the first place. The moderation procedures adopted in Queensland include this type (see p. 40).

Approaches to quality assurance in assessment

Turning now from procedures where the main purpose is quality control to those where it is quality assurance, the common feature of procedures in this category is that they attempt to increase dependability of teachers' assessments. They usually take place before the assessment is made but can operate in a *post hoc* fashion. In the latter case the quality assurance function is distinguished from one of quality control only by the use made of the information. For example, whilst reference tests are no longer used to adjust marks in public examination in the UK, they may be used to draw attention

> to those cases where the locally determined marks are different from what might be expected on the basis of the same candidates' performance on the national yardstick. Such cases can then be investigated in detail by visiting verifiers, who are in the best position to draw a distinction between two major possibilities: local interpretation of standards out of line with national ones, or a level of performance on the local component genuinely different from what was expected as a result of performance on the national yardstick (perhaps as a result of extra emphasis or reduced emphasis on the local component, in terms of time, interest or resources).
>
> (Nuttall and Thomas, 1993, p. 6)

As this passage indicates, quality assurance procedures have to be concerned with both validity and reliability and so the focus is on the opportunities for learning and assessment and on increasing shared understandings of assessment criteria and procedures. There is a considerable variation, however, in the extent to which these concerns can be addressed in a single approach. Thus the quality assurance procedures used in several cases comprise a combination of approaches. For the purpose of exemplifying possible procedures, however, the approaches used are considered separately.

Defining criteria for assessment

The provision of criteria to be applied in all schools by the government, in the form of statements of learning outcomes in the national curricula of England and Wales, Scotland and Northern Ireland, and the provision of national criteria for vocational qualifications by the National Council for Vocational Qualifications (NCVQ) in England and Wales and its counterpart in Scotland, the Scottish Vocational Education Council (SCOTVEC), were intended to provide a basis for uniformity in assessments made in the school, college or workplace. The 'intrinsic moderation' which is brought about by close specification of examination syllabuses and marking schemes, as in South Australia (see p. 45), is a further example.

However, the reliability of criterion-referenced, or competence-based, assessment depends upon the clarity and ease of application of the statements of performance. The familiar dilemma facing those who define criteria is that the more specific and unambiguous the statements are, the more numerous and the less meaningful in terms of the abilities and understandings which are the real educational aims. Conversely the more the statements reflect complex, and particularly higher level, learning outcomes the more difficult they are to use reliably in assessment. The approach to quality assurance of providing criteria is, therefore, often accompanied by a constant revision aimed at improving the specification of criteria, attempting to avoid the problems of being too general or too specific. Examples are changes made to the National Curriculum statements of attainment in response to the unmanageability of the curriculum for assessment purposes and the changes made to Scottish National Certificate performance criteria as part of a revision of quality assurance procedures (SCOTVEC, 1991). The provision and revision of criteria, whilst usually involving representatives of those who have to use them, is not open to negotiation with teachers and other users. Thus it is somewhat remote from influence by teachers and equally, of itself, weak in influence on teachers' assessments of individual students.

Exemplification

The provision of examples of pupils' work which has been assessed, preferably with a commentary on particular features used in making the judgement, enables abstract criteria to be made specific. Good examples also indicate the type of task which provides opportunity for pupils to develop and to make evident their achievement of skills and understanding. Examples include the Schools Examinations and Assessment Council's publications *Children's Work Assessed (KS1)* and *Pupils' Work Assessed (KS3)* (SEAC, 1991) and the proposed assessment handbook to accompany the New Zealand achievement initiative (see p. 39). Such examples can be used in group discussions similar to agreement trials (see below) but can also be used by a teacher individually. Unlike agreement trials, however, exemplification does not deal with work carried out in a context familiar to teachers and in that respect may have less impact on teachers' reflection on their own practice.

Approval of institutions/centres

This approach to quality assurance is a process by which the body responsible for certain awards approves an institution or centre as one which can provide the course or training and can carry out the assessment related to

these awards. Institutions or centres are visited, course or training documents are reviewed, qualifications of staff are vetted and resources are
inspected. Assessment procedures are included, although there may be
other moderation procedures required by the awarding body in relation to
quality control. Examples of this approach are the visitations which the
Council for National Academic Awards used to carry out in approving
courses and institutions and the 'quality auditing' of centres introduced by
SCOTVEC from 1992. The approval of a centre may have implications
for the locus of responsibility for ensuring reliability of assessments, since
in some cases this will be devolved to the institution or centre. It will also
affect the assessment process directly or indirectly by ensuring some
standardisation of procedures across institutions or centres.

Visits of verifiers or moderators

This refers to visits made to observe the way in which assessment is
carried out rather than to discuss products after the event, although in
certain circumstances the two may be combined. Examples include the
visits of moderators to schools during the administration of standard
tasks as part of National Curriculum Assessment (NCA) and visits of
verifiers to workplaces or colleges where National Vocational Qualifications (NVQ) assessments are being made. The emphasis is upon the
procedures being implemented and the way in which criteria are being
applied. Whilst the latter involves consideration of particular pieces of
work or performance, the purpose is to inform the interpretation of
criteria statements rather than to arrive at an agreed assessment in the
cases that happen to be discussed. In this connection, it has been reported that moderators rarely changed Key Stage 1 teachers' judgements during NCA visits in order to preserve teachers' confidence
(James and Conner, 1993). The intention is to influence the assessment
process and by doing so ensure greater reliability of assessment of students other than those whose performance was considered in the visit.

Group moderation

Also known as agreement panels, these are meetings of teachers or
lecturers at which examples of work are discussed, the purpose being to
arrive at shared understandings of the criteria in operation. The in-
service function is foremost and the benefit greatest when teachers feel
able to express their judgements and justify them openly, so that different conceptions and assumptions can be addressed. Membership may
be from one school or several and groups led by an appointed local

authority moderator or by a teacher. Persuasive arguments can be made for both inter-school and intra-school panel meetings; indeed both were proposed by the Northern Ireland Schools Examinations and Assessment Council (NISEAC) as part of the Northern Ireland national assessment arrangements (NISEAC, 1991). Inter-school meetings have a greater impact on reliability at the system level than intra-school meetings but are more costly.

Quality in moderation

Quality in moderation procedures can be considered using the same concepts of validity and reliability as for quality in assessment. In effect this would be saying that the approach(es) used would be the most relevant in relation to sources of variability (that is the most valid) and would have consistent and repeatable effects on different occasions (reliability). Although this application of validity and reliability has been pursued effectively in relation to secondary school examinations (SSABSA, 1988) it is perhaps rather too theoretical for our purposes here. (For example, very little information exists about the reliability of moderation procedures even when restricted to those used in such examinations.) Instead it seems useful to discuss differences in terms of those features which have been mentioned in describing them, mainly impact on process, on the product, on professional development, cost, type of control, range of evidence and timing. The particular combination of features which indicate quality will depend on the purpose and context of the assessment. *Thus we might define quality in moderation as the process which optimises the reliability of an assessment at a cost which is balanced by the benefits in terms of the purposes of the assessment and contributions to professional developments.*

In conclusion

This chapter has attempted to give an overview of the most commonly used forms of moderation, without dwelling on the details of the variants which also exist. The different approaches have been grouped according to their main function, as quality assurance or quality control, but there are other ways in which they can be categorised and compared as, for example, by whether their impact is at student, school or LEA level. We shall return in the final chapter to the matter of how they compare one with another on different dimensions and to the question of their effectiveness. At that point we shall be able to draw upon the many examples of moderation in practice given in Chapters 2 and 5 to 7.

References

Harlen, W., Gipps, C., Broadfoot, P. and Nuttall, D. (1992) Assessment and the improvement of education, *The Curriculum Journal*, Vol. 3, no. 3, pp. 215–30.

James, M. and Conner, C. (1993) Are reliability and validity achievable in National Curriculum Assessment? Some observations on moderation at key stage one, *The Curriculum Journal*, Vol. 4, no. 1, pp. 5–19.

Newbould, C. A. and Massey, A. J. (1979) *Comparability using a Common Element*, Test Development and Research Unit, Cambridge.

NISEAC (Northern Ireland School Examination and Assessment Council) (1991) *Pupil Assessment in Northern Ireland*, Advice to the Lord Belstead, Paymaster General, NISEAC, January 1991.

Nuttall, D. L. and Thomas, S. (1993) *Monitoring Procedures Based on Centre Performance Variables*, Report no. 11. A technical report published by the Employment Department's Methods Strategy Unit, Sheffield.

SCOTVEC (Scottish Vocational Education Council) (1991) *Quality Development Programme*, Policy Paper, SCOTVEC, Glasgow.

SEAC (School Examination and Assessment Council) (1991) *Children's Work Assessed (KS1)* and *Pupils' Work Assessed (KS3)*, SEAC, London.

SEC (Secondary Examinations Council) (1985) *Coursework Assessment in GCSE*, Working Paper 2, SEC, London.

Smith, G. A. (1978) *The JMB Experience of the Moderation of Internal Assessments* (occasional paper 38), Joint Matriculation Board, Manchester.

SSABSA (1988) *Information Booklet No. 2, Assessment and Moderation*, South Australia, SSABSA.

Wiliam, D. (1992) Some technical issues in assessment: a user's guide, *British Journal of Curriculum and Assessment*, Vol. 2, no. 3, pp. 11–20.

2

APPROACHES TO QUALITY ASSURANCE AND CONTROL IN SIX COUNTRIES

Patricia Broadfoot

Introduction

One of the great strengths of comparative educational research is that it can document contrasts between countries in the way that they seek to achieve similar ends. In so doing, it not only helps to illuminate complex relationships of cause and effect but it can also stimulate the questioning of existing practice (Crossley and Broadfoot, 1992). At a time when countries are actively seeking to 'borrow' policies and practices from each other (Phillips, 1991), the provision of comparative information in an analytical and systematic way is potentially an important avenue through which educational research can make an impact and thus contribute to the improvement of practice. Comparative studies also underline the equally important caution that all such differences are reflections of the culture that produced them and thus can never be simply translated from one cultural setting to another.

With these goals in mind, this chapter reviews the quality assurance and quality control practices of six countries: the USA, Germany, Sweden, France, New Zealand and Australia. These examples have been chosen in order to illustrate the considerable variety of practice which exists internationally and briefly to identify some of the key social factors which have led to these differences of approach. This identification of the aspects of particular national contexts which lie behind the commitment to certain assessment traditions and practices is in turn the

Copyright © 1994, Patricia Broadfoot

basis for generating a more general understanding of the key variables which need to be taken into account in any attempt to change such practice. This is the subject of the final part of the chapter.

Quality assurance and control in the USA

Educational assessment in the USA has been dominated from the earliest stages of its development by psychometric approaches (Berlak *et al.*, 1992). The invention of the multiple-choice test in 1914 and of optical mark readers for scoring such tests in 1955 facilitated the implementation of an approach in which testing became associated with a highly sophisticated technology, its scientific image justifying its establishment as a professional enterprise detached from teachers and the process of education itself (Madaus, 1993). In recent years the perceived limitations of this 'teacher-proof' external approach to assessment have fuelled the growth of the movement to introduce more 'authentic' forms of assessment which rely on a variety of classroom-based teacher assessment.

Many questions are now being raised in American assessment circles concerning the definition of assessment quality. The long-standing domination of reliability as a criterion of quality, linked as it is to issues concerning the impartiality of the assessment process, arguably reflected the American dream of an egalitarian society forged out of the cultural melting pot in which any individual could rise in accordance with their talent and effort. The recent poor showing of US educational standards in international comparisons, coupled with the need to promote the learning of more high-level intellectual skills, has led policy-makers to prioritise a different set of assessment agendas and, in particular, to identify assessment as a means of bringing about desired curriculum reform. In 1983 *A Nation at Risk* called for school systems to reconsider their curricula and to provide stringent accountability concerning standards in order to achieve the more valid and useful forms of learning it associated with more classroom-based 'authentic' assessment. Such 'authentic' assessment is likely to involve some combination of the 'three Ps' of performance, projects and portfolios. Baker, O'Neil and Linn (1991) summarise the attributes of the alternative assessment approaches now being developed on a widespread basis in the USA as including: 'the use of open-ended tasks; a focus on higher-order or complex skills; the employment of context-sensitive strategies; being performance-based, sometimes over an extended time period; involving either individual or group performance; and possibly involving a considerable degree of student choice' (p. 38).

Whilst not especially radical from a European perspective, the proposed introduction of a national system of examinations under the New Standards Project which would use this kind of approach is raising the question of moderation for perhaps the first time. As Baker *et al.* (1991) point out, comparability and hence, in our terms, quality control, has been assured in the past by empirical development of test items, standardised and secure administration and scoring practices, and the norming of tests on carefully selected populations. In reviewing the options for ensuring the comparability of alternative assessment (Table 2.1), they admit that all of the approaches have their weaknesses. A particular concern is the potential 'corruptibility' of the assessment process where teachers teach to the test (Shepard, 1991).

Table 2.1   Methods to address comparability of alternative assessments

Specification: the public description of performance standards to include task formats, content quality, cognitive demands, and scoring criteria. These specifications are used to guide and to assure quality of assessment development

Calibration: procedures for monitoring and adjusting scores of different raters to make them empirically comparable

Moderation: procedures to allow individuals to acquire shared understanding of performance standards

Training: a more direct form of moderation, where individuals learn to rate performance to agreed standards

Verification and audit: procedures to double-check scoring (and assessment content) to assure that appropriate assessment standards are met

Source: Baker, O'Neil and Linn (1991).

Now the New Standards Project (Tucker and Resnick, 1990) has brought these issues into sharp focus since the intention is to design a national examination system using 'authentic' assessment techniques, the results of which can be used for post-secondary school admission, by employers and for system accountability in providing a target for all aspiring high-school graduates. Ideas for providing comparability are variously called 'equating', 'anchoring', 'benchmarking', 'calibrating' or 'linking'. The current proposal is that there should be performance examinations, which are examinations that students prepare for in advance and take on a planned day or days under appropriate supervision, and a cumulative record of achievement which includes portfolios, exhibitions and projects. The proposed national system would rely on the calibration of local or regional examinations with a national 'anchor' exam or national standards embodied in tasks. The direction of current thinking is illustrated in a recent paper by Linn (1991). Model 1 proposes a national anchor exam for a sample of students in each grade level to verify individual standards assessed by regional or local examinations. Model 2 uses some element of a national exam which local examinations and Model 3 has no common elements but instead would use visiting marking teams to cross-moderate between districts.

Most of these approaches to moderation are already familiar in Europe and, as Madaus and Kellaghan (1991) suggest, established European practice may well have an influence on US assessment practice. However, Madaus and Kellaghan distinguish the long-standing emphasis of European examinations on *content*, with the associated assumption that examinations will heavily constrain content, from the current US preoccupation with promoting *skills* and suggest that this is likely to sustain continuing differences in approach. Madaus and Kellaghan further distinguish the different assessment traditions of Europe and the USA in terms of the level of public confidence in teachers who in Europe are trusted to determine and grade examination questions. Because of this they suggest, in Europe, far from being separated from it, assessment is integrally related to the curriculum. However, within this global distinction between the very different traditions of the USA and Europe, there are some important differences within the European Union itself which are worthy of further exploration.

Quality assurance and control in Germany

The defining context of German education, especially in the former West Germany, is the right of the individual *Länder* to make and implement its own educational policy. Hence there is considerable variation from one province to another. There is now, however, agreement between the *Länder* over broad common conditions for the structure, conduct and subject composition of the key education qualification – the eighteen-plus *Abitur* – and major qualifications are typically accepted as equivalent between the *Länder*. The current pattern of the *Abitur* was laid down by agreement at the Standing Conference of *Länder* Ministers of Education (*Kultusminister Konferenz* (KMK)) in 1972 and most recently updated in 1988.

The other defining characteristic of German educational provision is its strongly centralised character. In most *Länder* the curriculum is centrally determined according to specific statements of what is to be learned at each age level. Partly because of the very strongly centralised control of content there has been little national concern over standards, and the assessment procedures remain very largely the responsibility of teachers even for certification and selection purposes with minimal external intervention. This is partly because the use of a six-point mark scale (*notenskala*), ranging from 1 ('very good') to 6 ('irretrievable failure') is a well-known feature of German education and is well understood by all associated with German schooling. The formal assessment which is made at the end of primary school is based on continuous assessment from the beginning of the penultimate year onwards based on half-yearly marks for all subjects of the curriculum plus descriptive comments on the child's attitudes, adjustment to work and to other people. Halfway through the final primary year the class teacher prepares a report (*gutachten*) which describes the pupils' achievement, learning ability and independence and makes a recommendation concerning which kind of secondary school the child is suited to. This report forms the basis of the secondary school's decision whether to accept a pupil.

If the pupil is assessed as being suited to neither grammar nor technical high school, a parent may wish to challenge the assessment. In this event there is provision for a further assessment (*probeunterricht*) in which for three days a child becomes part of a group of children in the same situation and is taught by other teachers and given tests by them. These new teachers produce a second assessment. In some *Länder* the parents are allowed to overrule the primary school assessment, in others they are not. Whilst there is obviously a degree of anxiety produced where key selection divisions depend on a two-year process of continuous assessment, this approach to assessment stresses the key role of the teacher as a 'professional assessor' such that no further moderation or control mechanism is needed.

It is quite surprising that the legitimacy of the traditional marking system in German education is not underpinned by any mechanism for acquainting teachers with standards in other schools. There is now some evidence of concern within the system in this respect in recognition that teachers may well not have a good grasp of other schools' standards.

Access to upper secondary education and higher levels of vocational education depends on the acquisition of an appropriate leaving certificate. The assessment is typically made on the basis of assessments made within the school including systematic half-yearly reports and discussions among the teachers of a class. These reports are based on formal internal school tests. Whilst these tests are carefully constructed and pupils are warned of the time and content of them in advance, they are within the control of individual teachers.

Assessment for the *Abitur* score is based on a combination of examinations and continuous assessment during Years 12 and 13. Where an examination mark deviates significantly from coursework assessment, the student must take an oral in that subject, or he/she can request an oral in the hope of marginally raising an examination mark. The total *Abitur* score is calculated by combining results gained in various courses during the last two years of schooling with results of the final examinations.

> These coursework marks depend on a series of formal written tests as well as on the teacher's assessment of 'Sonstige Mitarbeit', other work done for the class. In a remarkably complex way the traditional six-point scale is at this stage converted to a fifteen-point scale (by adding plus and minus marks to each of the five levels, a mark of 6 counting as zero) and marks in different types of course are weighted, for example (points gained in advanced courses in Year 12 are multiplied by 2). The number of points awarded for the actual final examinations is less than half the maximum points total of between 800 and 900. After the 'Abitur' examination the points total is converted by an agreed conversion scale to the familiar and better understood six-point scale, although now with decimal points added. The ideal mark of '1' is sometimes achieved.
>
> (Sutherland, 1993, p. 57)

Although there are some in which the questions are centrally set and presented to schools as an unseen examination, in most of the *Länder* the *Arbitur* questions are set by the candidate's own teacher. At the beginning of the year the teacher draws up two or three sets of questions, with a commentary about how these have been taught and what responses are expected. The central authority will then normally choose one set of questions and inform the school which is to be used. Teachers are provided with national and *Länder*-produced guidance to help them in the generation of test questions.

Typically the examination papers are marked by the candidate's own teacher and then second marked by a colleague from the same department. The school is responsible for quality control in checking that the administration of the *Abitur* has been in strict accordance with national requirements laid down by the KMK. Thus, except for some external checking of samples of scripts, quality assurance and quality control in Germany is very largely part of the professional responsibility of teachers.

In their report published in 1987 entitled *Education in the Federal Republic of Germany: Aspects of Curriculum and Assessment*, HMI record how cheap to run the German assessment model is without the elaborate paraphernalia of external involvement characteristic of the UK – a point also made by Sadler (1991) concerning the internal assessment used in Queensland, Australia, which he estimates saves two-thirds of the cost of an external assessment system. The relatively low-key German approach to comparability may be because the high-stakes point of the system, namely the *Abitur*, was traditionally a qualifying examination for university with all successful students being entitled to enrol. As increasing numbers of university departments have introduced a *numerus clausus*, concerns about the comparability of the assessments made, particularly between *Länder*, have become more overt.

In relation to the other 'high-stakes' point of the system, namely the eleven-plus-type selection, again this was not a major problem in the past as many German parents did not aspire for their children to go to the gymnasium. The increase in parental aspirations which might have caused a problem has been matched by a softening in the allocation procedures as described above, so that the elevation of the assessment into an excessively high-stakes mode has been avoided.

Thus quality assurance in Germany is essentially a professional matter. The structural purposes and long-standing legitimacy of the procedures in use, coupled with the high traditional status of teachers in Germany, combine to make unnecessary any more formal provision for comparability: 'At a time when doubts have been expressed in Britain about the validity of coursework, it is worth noting the emphasis which the Germans place on such forms of assessment including response in class as well as written work' (Neather, 1993, p. 21).

Quality assurance and control in Sweden

Like that in Germany, Swedish education provision has traditionally been characterised by a high degree of central control at both school and higher education levels. Although a margin of decentralisation has recently been introduced there is still a centralised curriculum. However, the approach to moderation in Sweden is very different, emphasising a bureaucratic, statistical moderation approach. This is perhaps because of the well-known Swedish preoccupation with equality and hence, as in the USA, with the need for transparent reliability.

At the end of each three-year stage of the nine-year compulsory school which provides comprehensive education for all children from age seven to sixteen, teachers are provided with nationally produced but voluntary diagnostic tests. The aim of these tests is to identify whether students have reached the minimum competency required in the core subjects of Swedish and maths at the end of each stage. Similar tests are also used in the upper secondary vocational lines. The tests are designed to provide teachers with information so that they can compare their pupils' results against the national average. One of the effects of the tests is to focus teachers on the essential competences to be acquired, and the tests are deliberately designed to do this. Where inadequacies are identified in this way, teachers are expected to provide remedial support.

Entry to the chosen course in upper secondary school is now not subject to any formal hurdle and students are assessed at the end of the basic school only on the traditional five-point marking scale. Comparability of marking between schools is assured by the use of centrally generated tests, the results of which are used to calibrate teachers' own marks. The nationally normed test results received from the schools are analysed and (some revised) scales determined in order that teachers can compare their own pupils' achievement with those of other teachers throughout the country and use this information in giving marks to individual pupils within their classes.

A similar test for upper secondary school is compulsory for all the main subjects. The tests are published each year and therefore annually produced. Teachers adjust the marks students achieve on their own tests, set in each subject during the year, in order to correspond with the results achieved by their classes in the national scaling tests. The tests, which are open to public scrutiny and which have a clear effect on the grades which students can achieve on leaving upper secondary school, are 'high stakes' and exert a not inconsiderable wash-back effect on the curriculum. This is taken into account when the tests are devised and considerable efforts are made to make sure the tests reinforce the whole range of skills embodied in the curriculum. The assumption is that the average mark awarded to the country as a whole should be 3 – the mid-point of the scale – with 7 per cent at each extreme (marks of 1 and 5), 24 per cent in the intermediate bands (marks of 2 and 4) and 38 per cent in the central bands (a mark of 3) (Sutherland, 1993).

Some experiments have recently been undertaken in vocational subjects using a modular approach with a pass/fail rating. But under the present system such assessments cannot be taken into the overall calculations of marks obtained. This has the effect of further devaluing vocational subjects.

Since 1991 all students have been able to opt for selection for higher education based not on moderated school marks but on scores achieved on an alternative test which, like the American Scholastic Aptitude Test which it resembles, is a multiple-choice test. This was originally provided for adult entry to higher education but is now taken by some 40 per cent of school students. Marks are converted to standardised scores by means of statistical moderation.

Thus in Sweden, as in Germany, there is very considerable emphasis on quality assurance in assessment through developing teachers' expertise in assessment and then trusting them to carry it out. Unlike in Germany, however, it is more of a 'belt and braces' approach in that quality control procedures in the form of a scaling test are also involved – most particularly at the key decision points in a student's career. Not surprisingly, this approach causes considerable unhappiness among teachers forced to change their marks and can seem arbitrary in use – a problem that the government has sought to address in part at least by providing more guidance for teachers concerning the assessment process, such as that on marks and marking in the upper secondary school, published by the National Board of Education in 1990. It also reinforces a norm-referenced approach to assessment. It is clearly not universally popular with students either, as increasing numbers opt for the alternative multiple-choice test.

Quality assurance and control in France

France has many similarities with Germany in the association of the traditionally high-status upper secondary teachers with a strong emphasis on professional responsibility in assessment. However, the tensions caused by the innovation of continuous assessment alongside the more familiar external examinations, illustrate the heavier reliance that has traditionally been placed on externally set examinations in France. Indeed, Kreeft (1990) characterises France as a classic example of an external examining system. For example, the first formal assessment – the *Diplôme National du Brevet* – which is taken at the end of *collège* before proceeding to the *lycée*, is based on the combination of an external examination in French, maths, history and geography and on the results of continuous assessment. It is something of an anomaly, because, whilst the locally set examination is rigorously standardised, there is little or no moderation of the continuous assessment awarded by the school which tends to be overgenerous in its marking. Even so, in many places, the percentage of students achieving average marks is too low so that the whole distribution is moderated up to ensure 20 per cent of candidates achieve an acceptable standard. This results in inequalities between different departments and penalisation of the more rigorous, leading to widespread doubts about the value of the results (Caroff, 1991).

It is not without significance that despite repeated calls to reform the prestigious eighteen-plus *baccalauréat* examination into a more school-based examination, not least because of the enormous cost of teacher time in externally examining what is now a huge number of students, students, parents and teachers continue to give very strong support to the notion of an anonymous external examination as a guarantee of equality against the influence of teachers' values and schools of different status. Yet despite this rhetoric it is widely accepted that there are variations between different subjects and different geographical areas in current procedures. These variations have become more acute since 1966 when the responsibility for the examination was entirely devolved to the *recteur d'academie*. Now in each *academie* there is an elaborate committee structure and a small permanent staff, who, with the aid of a computer, must set and mark over a hundred different examination papers for something over a million candidates. Although the 1983 Prost Report on the reform of the *lycée* argues for a considerably increased measure of continuous assessment, little progress has been made in this respect. In 1991 Lionel Jospin again tried to introduce continuous assessment in the *baccalauréate* but without much success.

Continuous assessment is currently most widely being used in the *lycées professionnels* with students studying for the more vocational *baccalauréat professionel*. In these institutions, final examinations and marks have been abandoned for some time in favour of teaching based on detailed course objectives with evaluation checklists of the detailed assessment criteria within a framework of modular courses. Teachers using these procedures, however, complain that the continuing formality of their role and the time involved for continuous assessment is not recognised, and while 80 per cent of senior staff support continuous assessment as providing for more valid assessment, many teachers fear being vulnerable to outside pressures and being accused of favouritism under this system. They also doubt the national value of a qualification in which teachers have a say in the results of their own students. This underlines the fact that no non-traditional moderation procedures appear to have developed to support this kind of assessment. It also marks a stark contrast to Germany where this would be regarded as normal.

Like Germany, France does emphasise the professional dimension in promoting assessment quality. This is well illustrated in the procedures for student certification. In terms of national assessment, France has had since 1974 a national programme for evaluating students' results. The tests used are a mixture of multiple-choice and structured written questions and are marked by teachers according to strict guidelines to ensure comparability. However, since these are only sample surveys they are low stakes. More recently, in 1989, these monitoring surveys have been complemented by an annual comprehensive evaluation of the attainment in French and mathematics of all students in third-year primary and first-year secondary school. The tests are conducted in the second week of the school year and are based on four twenty-five-minute tests of mathematics and French which are marked according to standardised coding guidelines so that teachers can analyse class results for which purposes they are provided with a software package. Parents are provided with information about their own child's results and the programme also has an important summative dimension in that aggregated results are published nationally so that parents, teachers and headteachers can compare their results against national norms. However, there is no attempt to compare school and school – such information being held confidentially to guard against any market orientation developing. The tests are therefore low stakes and no further moderation of the teacher's marking of this essentially diagnostic enterprise is required. Rather the goal is quality assurance – to encourage the best possible internal, professional assessment practice.

Thus with its traditionally high measure of central control of the system, the issue of comparability in France has not been as significant as in some other countries. As with the *Abitur* in Germany, the traditional right of access to higher education to all holders of the *baccalauréat* may have had some influence in this, although the advent of a *numerus clausus* in popular faculties is certainly raising the stakes in some *baccalauréat filières*. There is a very considerable wastage after the first year of university and the *propédétique* examination which also helps to lower the stakes of assessment during the course of schooling. In France, the notion that all schools are equal and the resolute refusal, *de jure* at least until recently, to recognise that schools might differ from each other in terms of the standards produced, has also contributed to reducing the significance of moderation as a formal issue. Undoubtedly the establishment of the *baccalauréat* examination for nearly two centuries since its foundation in 1808 contributes enormously to its legitimacy. This is both a strength – in that it tends to reduce potential pressure for apparently more effective quality control procedures – and a weakness – in that it is very hard to bring about any kind of change.

The two final examples in this chapter provide further contrasts to the American and European traditions in describing two countries – New Zealand and Australia – where there is strong influence of British traditions coupled with a range of idiosyncratic local developments. These have combined to produce some rather different approaches to quality assurance and control.

Quality assurance and control in New Zealand

Perhaps because of the strong British influence, New Zealand education has long been dominated by external assessments. Indeed, until recently pupils were subject to an examination in each of the final three years of secondary schooling: the School Certificate taken at the end of Year 10, sixth-form certificate at Year 11 and bursary at Year 12. School Certificate has traditionally been a school-based examination moderated by an externally devised scaling test, not dissimilar to the Swedish model. This test has been the bone of much contention, not only because of its arbitrary impact on School Certificate but because it is used to constrain schools in their allocation of marks in the following year. This scaling test was abolished in 1992 and indeed the whole system of formal qualifications has now been overtaken by a major national initiative – the National Qualifications Framework – designed to move the system from a norm-referenced examination system to a system which assesses achievement against recognised standards. This initiative involves a change to unit-based learning and to modular assessment. The National Certificate units will cover a spectrum through general subjects to clearly vocationally oriented subjects. Existing school subjects will be transformed into general units.

Given that all qualifications in the post-compulsory stages of education, although not, at present, degree and post-degree level, will be in a common framework and system of organisation, this will represent a radical change in the basis of quality assurance and control in the awarding of qualifications. The New Zealand Qualifications Authority (NZQA) has taken the decision to devolve quality management progressively to providers as an integral part of their delivery of services, with quality audits by the authority (NZQA, 1991a).

It is envisaged that quality assurance will be based on: registration, a process which ensures that private training establishments meet fundamental standards of delivery which safeguard their clients; approval, the formal recognition of units of learning and groups of units which make up qualifications by the authority; and accreditation, the formal recognition that a provider is capable of delivering units to the standard specified. The responsibility for the quality of education and training lies first and foremost with providers in partnership with their clients and the role of the qualifications authority is envisaged as one of ensuring that providers have quality control and assurance processes in place. This requires quality audit, the independent checking of the quality processes of providers. Quite what all this will mean in practice has not yet been worked out in detail (NZQA, 1991b, 10) but two documents issued in 1992 by NZQA illustrate the high profile of moderation issues in the development of the new system and the possibility that there will be devolution of the responsibility of providing for quality assurance and control.

The system already requires that registered units have clearly expressed performance criteria. Accredited providers must have quality management systems including policies and procedures that cover teaching and administration as well as assessment and reporting and provide for ongoing evaluation of the quality of such procedures. They will be subject to external audit.

National moderation can be provided by NZQA itself, a national professional or industrial association, providers or private consultants. Alternatively moderation can be locally conducted on the basis of criteria laid down by a national standards body if they can confirm that local arrangements meet the criteria. Twelve possible approaches to moderation are offered including: the use of exemplars and the benchmark materials; recognition of 'expert' assessors; external written examinations; statistical moderation; common assessment tasks and reference tests; item banks; distance moderators; external assessors (to assess locally); external moderators with site visits (to confirm local assessments); external moderators with panel meetings (moderator in charge); consensus panels (group decisions); and panel networks (NZQA, 1992).

Two other recent developments relate to the use of assessment in national monitoring:

The achievement initiative

This initiative centres on the development of clear learning outcomes, particularly in the basic subjects of English, mathematics, science and technology.

> The national curriculum objectives will be expressed as learning outcomes and will include descriptions of the achievement standards which can reasonably be expected of students at particular levels of learning. The objectives will show progression and continuity of learning for the years of compulsory schooling and beyond. The statements will be sufficiently specific for sound assessment and monitoring to occur. They will not, however, be so specific as to limit the local school and classroom teacher in their response to the learning needs of students.
>
> (*Education Gazette*, 1991)

The development of these clearly defined levels of achievement will also include the development of assessment exemplars which will provide guidance to classroom teachers in making appropriate judgements about their student's achievement. The levels of achievement are intended to help teachers in providing clear profiles of individual student achievement for parental reporting. It is intended that for each of the core subjects a small assessment document or handbook will be produced to support the draft curriculum document. This is to provide a practical guide for teachers based on assessment exemplars and procedures included in the curriculum document. It will include such things as the assessment context, appropriate assessment instruments and methods and a sample of student responses to guide teachers and show how the actual classroom assessment of achievement in a subject relates to the curriculum statements defining the levels of achievement. The achievement initiative, which will involve the creation of a national item bank of assessment material, will provide schools with materials to administer to students at the beginning of the year as the students embark on a new cycle in their learning. This development is to be accompanied by a shift in emphasis in the Education Review Office (equivalent to inspection) from evaluation of the achievement of a school's broad charter objectives concerning, for example, equal opportunities or reporting to parents, to one where monitoring is more directly against the objectives embodied in the achievement initiative.

National monitoring

It has been agreed that national monitoring, probably at the ages of eight, ten and twelve which are natural transition points in the New Zealand system, will be implemented with a sample of around 5 per cent of students at each age level. The assessment will be developed by external agencies and operated by these agencies along the lines of other national monitoring systems.

Thus it would seem that New Zealand is in the process of moving from a moderation system based on closed statistical procedures to one based partly on criterion-referenced assessment coupled with quality assurance procedures operated within the learning institutions themselves. This will be combined with a professional model involving a reliance on the increased professionalism and expertise of teachers in the administration of national assessment. In this respect, New Zealand has strong parallels with France and to an extent with Scotland. It remains to be seen, however, how significant these various initiatives will be in breaking down the traditional dominance within the educational system of the very high-stakes bursary and scholarship examinations, with their reliance on traditional formal external examining procedures and traditional forms of quality control.

Quality assurance and control in Australia

Each state in Australia has its own education system and only three are included here to illustrate their contrasting system of moderation. As a general rule formal provision for quality assurance and quality control in assessment is focused on the upper secondary school stage and particularly entrance to higher education. Moderation in the three states to be discussed here is related to entrance to tertiary education and is carried out either because of the emphasis on school-based assessment (Queensland) where there is no external school-leaving examination or if there is an external certificating examination, statistical moderation is used to scale scores to provide a single aggregate for entrance to university. In some cases there is both group moderation and scaling to produce a ranking of students.

Queensland

There have been no external examinations in Queensland for twenty years and assessment is therefore all based in school (Baumgart and McBryde, 1992). The first formal assessment point is at Year 10. Formerly the Junior Certificate, the school-issued certification and exit statement is now absorbed into a student portfolio which was introduced in 1989 for all Year 10 pupils in state schools and 1990 for non-state schools. This portfolio shows the academic and personal achievements of the student and includes documentation concerning his or her abilities, skills and interests, which provides a comprehensive picture of the student's accomplishments, attributes and involvement. Given the essentially descriptive nature of the Year 10 documentation, there is no move to provide formally for quality control of the data although efforts are being made on quality assurance to help teachers improve the quality of their assessment procedures.

At Year 12, however, whilst the assessments are still school based, there is considerably more attention given to external moderation in the critically important context of university entrance qualifications. School-based assessment is on a five-point rating scale still moderated by panels of teachers who review the quality of work from different schools, that is through consensus moderation. A separate procedure is used to scale the school-based achievement scores across subjects and across schools. This is done in order to calculate for each pupil an aggregate score and to compile an order of merit list for allocating places in higher education. All students who wanted to go to tertiary education took a scaling test: the Australian Scholastic Aptitude Test (ASAT). This test was given to all students and used to scale scores awarded by teachers first within schools, and then across schools (this device of using a common test as a scaling device is widely used in Australia, and is further discussed below). The scaling is designed to allow their achievements in different subjects to be projected on to a common scale; with the aggregate scores for all students in a school yielding a distribution with the mean and standard deviation corresponding to those of the ASAT scores. This tertiary entrance score (TES) was convenient for universities because it allowed them a very simple (some might say simplistic) form of selecting students without referencing to additional information. From 1986 the school-based assessment has been on a criterion-referenced model with defined performance criteria linked to the five-point scale. The system of criterion-referenced assessment also involves group moderation.

The latest arrangement following the Viviani Review (1990) involves the use of school-based assessment with the single TES replaced by a Student Education Profile containing a wider number of scales to be used in different combinations for selection into different university courses. This is significant as a move away from the single aggregate score so typical of higher education selection arrangements in Australia. Certification at the end of senior school thus has two levels: the Senior Certificate records performance in the final two years of schooling as measured by school-based assessment. Reporting is again on a five-point scale together with results on a Core Skills Test. The Core Skills Test is new and it is given to all Year 12 students. The Core Skills Test maps on to the curriculum and involves four separate tests: two multiple choice, one essay and one short response assessing cross-curricular skills; the core skills are also reported on a five-point scale. The second certificate, called the Tertiary Entrance Statement, provides a rank order for students for university selection. The students are given an overall position (OP) which is a single aggregate (as with the old TES) but on a more detailed twenty-five-point scale derived by averaging, with equal weight, scaled scores on the best five subjects for each student (the school-based assessment is scaled by using the core skills test result) but in addition each pupil is given up to five positions in separate fields. The field skills are: extended written expression; short written communication in English or a foreign language; basic numeracy; complex problem-solving; substantial practical performance. Normally students will get a field position score in two or three of the five fields. The idea is that universities will be obliged to look at the students' overall profile of results rather than just relying on the single aggregate score.

At lower levels of schooling, assessment of students is the professional responsibility of teachers and not subject to formal quality control. Thus we can see that in Queensland the context for moderation is that of tertiary entrance with the approach a mixture of statistical scaling and group moderation. The central concerns are the need to provide for comparability in a system which is heavily dependent on school-based assessment and questions over the validity of scaling to produce a single aggregate score. One anxiety about the new system in Queensland is that the moderated/scaled result is going to be fed back to the candidate. This has not happened before and there is some concern that it will lead to far greater emphasis being put on to the preparation for the core skills test.

New South Wales

In New South Wales students are assessed for the School Certificate at the end of Year 10 and Higher School Certificate (HSC) in Year 12. A state where certification procedures have traditionally been dominated by external examinations, the Board of Studies introduced a greater measure of school-based assessment in 1990 to provide students, parents and employers with more detail concerning achievement. External control of standards will be sustained through the continued use of an external reference test in English, mathematics and science. The results of this test are used to allocate a range of grades to each school. The school then awards these grades to students on the basis of their performance on the school's own assessment programme. In the three tested subjects, state-wide distributions of 10 per cent A, 20 per cent B, 40 per cent C, 20 per cent D and 10 per cent E) are applied. From 1991 all other subjects have been graded A to E, though on the basis of performance descriptors issued to schools rather than on the results of an external reference test. These performance descriptors, including course-specific descriptors – elementary to excellent – will be printed with the grades on the Year 10 record of achievement, for example:

> A – A grade indicating excellent achievement in the course. The student has an extensive knowledge and understanding of the course content and can readily apply this knowledge. In addition, the student has achieved a high level of competence in the processes and skills of the course and can apply these skills to new situations.
>
> (Australian Cooperative Assessment Program Newsletter,
> 1990, p. 2)

The intention has been to encourage teachers to apply criterion-, rather than norm-referenced standards – an aim which will be helped by there being no requirement for a fixed state-wide normal distribution.

In Year 12, however, the results on the HSC are scaled to produce a tertiary entrance score (TES), an aggregate single score which is used for tertiary entrance as in the Queensland system. However, students do not take a common reference test for scaling purposes, the scaling is done instead on an iterative system using the unbiased mean grade system or the UBMT (unbiased mean total). For example, if English is the subject under consideration, the UBMT for any candidate taking English is the sum of the grades obtained in all other subjects attempted, divided by the number of those subjects, or the mean grade in all other subjects attempted, that is minus English. This is therefore a strong version of moderation using statistical scaling.

The HSC involves an element of school-based assessment, commonly 50 per cent of the marks. From 1986 the school-based mark and the examination mark were reported separately; since 1988 the certificate has also included a report of the combined marks in decile bands. The scaling process was also used to produce a mean and standard deviation for each group of students in the school-based assessment with the same mean and standard deviation as obtained by the group in the external examination. Originally this scaling involved a linear transformation and it was thought that 'examiners and/or schools on occasion sought to modify the shape of the distribution to advantage some students' (Baumgart and McBryde, 1992, p. 6). Thus the system has moved to one of area transformation of scores rather than linear transformation of scores.

Calculation of the TES has produced regular problems and the scaling of community languages has been particularly difficult. In 1987 the Board of Senior Secondary Studies (the examination board) removed itself from the production of the TES and left it to the universities. Thus, currently, scaling across subjects has been abandoned and scores for each candidate for each course are reported raw without any attempt to adjust for the nature of the candidature. For one year all universities except the University of Sydney used a TES formed without scaling across subjects, but currently all universities use a system to produce a TES based on scaled scores across subjects (the current situation is that a TES is calculated first, and then a tertiary entrance rank (TER) is reported in percentage form in steps of 0.05).

The TES has been based on the best ten units offered by the student unless particular departments or universities require some unit of the curriculum to be included. This has meant that in the past, for example in 1991, 94 per cent of medical students and 45 per cent of law students entered the University of Sydney from the HSC with four maths units out of their ten on the HSC, while fewer than half of these students offered English at all in their TES. The current proposal is that there be some specification about which ten units be used for the TES including at least one unit of English and one unit from each of other areas of the core curriculum; not more than six units from any one field of study. In short they are moving towards a core curriculum to be included for tertiary entrance.

Thus in New South Wales the key focus for quality assurance and control is that of tertiary entrance. The approach to providing this is almost entirely that of statistical scaling and the issues are again to do with the validity of producing an aggregate score. Although there is an element of school-based assessment there is no group moderation process. Nevertheless,

> while the statistical scaling procedures used for the New South Wales HSC do not allow for teachers to be involved in moderation, involvement in the marking procedures is reported by many Head Teachers (of subject departments) as a highly valuable professional development activity for teachers of senior students. The experience of marking examination papers of students from across the state provides teachers with an idea of appropriate 'standards' such that when these teachers work on setting school based assessment tasks the following year they have a good understanding of the requirements of the Board of Studies.
>
> (Nelson, 1993, p. 1)

Like other states, New South Wales is currently concerned to introduce more extensive quality assurance procedures in schools. The Quality Assurance School reviews include a concern with the assessment and reporting practices in a school – a part of its aim is to help schools improve in this respect. Nevertheless, as an editorial in the *Sydney Morning Herald* (1993) makes clear, New South Wales is firmly committed to external assessment as the key to quality: 'the intention behind the reforms . . . was to create a fairer, more efficient and effective school system. In New South Wales this was done by empowering individual schools at the expense of the previously dominant central bureaucracy, the HSC examination, though was kept as the credential focus of the system.'

South Australia

Between 1978 and 1989 South Australia state schools issued a document to all school-leavers – the School Leaver Statement. In 1990 this was replaced by the Student Achievement Record (SAR) as the only official document issued to all school-leavers. The record details both formal academic achievements and non-formal activities. There is a composite report by three teachers on the way in which a student used language in a range of subjects plus teachers' comments on individual subjects. This school-verified statement of achievement fits inside a Personal Portfolio of documents concerning a wide range of student activities and achievements. When students reach Year 12 their achievements will be publicly certified through the South Australia Certificate of Education, but this is intended to be seen as an integral part of the SAR and portfolio. Teachers are provided with training and support materials to help them produce these records but there is no external monitoring.

There are two modes of assessment in Year 12 in South Australia. For university entrance the dominant mode has been examinations from what was called the Public Examinations Board (SSABSA, 1988). This group of subjects assessed by external examination are known as the PES (public examination subject) group; however, in the 1970s alternative curricula and syllabuses were developed for a secondary school certificate with no external examinations. These were assessed through school-based assessment and became known as SAS (school-assessed subjects). Thus there are two separate forms of assessment: SAS and PES. There is currently an attempt to merge the two forms and to equalise the status between them. PES results were reported only in a scaled norm-reference form whereas SAS results were untreated. The Senior Secondary Assessment Board of South Australia (SSABSA) is moving towards a new system of reporting subject achievement scores; each subject will be classified by the nature of the subject itself rather than by the assessment mode (that is not by PES or SAS). In every subject, teachers' assessments of student achievement will contribute to the overall assessment results. Currently teachers' assessments contribute 100 per cent in SAS and 50 per cent in PES although not all subjects in the latter have such a high proportion of teacher assessment. The current proposals are that all assessment designs must allow between 25 per cent and 100 per cent weighting for the teachers' assessment. Because of the extent of school-based assessment SSABSA has developed both visitation and group moderation systems which are well developed and have become a powerful instrument of professional development for teachers. Under the new proposals all measures of student achievement provided by teachers for this certificate will be moderated by SSABSA.

SSABSA (1988) identifies four systems of moderation. Their definition of moderation is 'a process in which external procedures are applied to the results of assessments of achievement in order to establish and/or maintain standards in a particular subject so that the quality of student achievement in that subject can be fairly judged' (p. 8).

(1) *Intrinsic moderation.* This occurs through the standard setting in an external examination system; using a common set of syllabus

objectives, the examination is set and marking schemes devised. Using a team approach the examiners mark the scripts on the basis of this marking system, i.e. the moderation is achieved through the setting and marking of the examination. 'The results of external examinations need no further subject moderation and are held to be self moderated' (SSABSA, 1988, p. 8).

(2) *Visitation moderation.* This is when visiting experts (moderators) apply a common set of criterion rules across the work of students in a number of classes to moderate teachers' assessments.

(3) *Group moderation.* This is the moderation of teachers' assessments by the common or consensus judgements of a group of teachers guided by a moderator.

(4) *Statistical moderation.* This is where teachers' assessments are moderated by the statistical application of a different but common assessment result which is used as a standard. In South Australia the results of a SSABSA external examination are used as the standard to moderate the results of teachers' assessments of the same student in that subject.

In South Australia moderation is in relation to certification at the end of secondary school (rather than strictly for selection to university). There is a considerable amount of group and visiting moderation in order to ensure comparability across schools. This is largely for the school-assessed subjects; there is also a form of statistical moderation for the public-examined subjects in order to moderate the teacher assessment part with the examined part. Current developments aim to bring together the two forms of assessment and to moderate each piece of information using the most appropriate method of moderation for that particular part.

Thus, as Withers (1992) points out, Australian 'school-based systems have much to teach others when it comes to protecting the validity of the system and the reliability of assessments made within it, at the same time as protecting the rights of individuals' (p. 17). He argues that in Australia comparability of school-based programmes depends on a combination of devolution of responsibility for assessment design and conduct to teachers who are given appropriate training, plus moderation provided for by common syllabuses and a combination of in-school, district-wide and system-wide meetings to ensure common standards and understanding. By comparison, Withers suggests, statistical moderation is arbitrary and not professionally supportive.

Australian experience thus provides a number of paradoxes. At the forefront of school-based moderation, it is also at the mercy of the arbitrary tertiary entrance score. The growing public confidence in teachers as assessors is squarely matched by reactionary forces within higher education. It is ironic that though these latter institutions have traditionally had no system of external moderation equivalent to the British system of external examining, they represent the major source of resistance to the implementation of more enlightened forms of quality assurance and control in schools.

Overview

Quality assurance procedures which are concerned with the quality of the process of assessment and quality control which is primarily concerned with the products of assessment both need to be judged in terms of their contribution to reliability and validity. Perhaps even more important, however, is the issue of utility and how far the assessment procedures being used contribute to, or inhibit, the achievement of national educational goals. Although overpolarised, Tables 2.2 and 2.3 illustrate the considerable variety that exists in each of the systems mentioned across different courses and levels of education. Given the major changes currently taking place in some systems, they summarise some of the important differences that have been described.

Table 2.2 Approaches to quality assurance

	Defining criteria	Accreditation of institutions/ centres	Visits of verifiers	Agreement panels
USA	*		*	*
Germany		*		*
Sweden				
France				
New Zealand	*	*	*	
Australia	*			*

Table 2.3 Approaches to quality control

	Reference/ scaling tests	Inspection of samples by post	Inspection of samples by visits	External examining	Appeals	Panel review
USA		*		*		*
Germany					*	
Sweden	*			*	*	
France				*	*	
New Zealand	*	*		*	*	
Australia	*	*	*	*	*	*

The origin of moderation procedures was the concern that assessment data should be meaningful; that like any other language, the code of grades or marks should represent an equivalent reality in terms of the standard achieved, whether it be between different subjects, different students or different institutions. Moderation is thus closely bound both with notions of utility and of fairness for individuals and for institutions. However, this international review has revealed many tensions in the achievement of such goals. It is apparent that in some countries at least the powerful voice of tradition and associated assumptions and the all important need for public credibility are together inhibiting the development of quality assurance and control procedures more suited to the achievement of the system's goals. Thus norm-referenced scaling procedures designed to rank students for selection continue to be imposed on systems which seek to develop more inclusive, criterion-referenced qualifications. The continued high status of external written examinations inhibits the effective pursuit of skills and competencies not amenable to such assessment. Qualifications which do involve more suitable forms of assessment continue to be regarded as of lower status. The valuable personal and professional development which can accrue for both teachers and students from being involved in making assessments (Sadler, 1989) is sacrificed to the apparently greater rigour of externally managed assessment.

But as one recent English research project into moderation has found (Shaw and Radnor, 1993), despite being promised no pay-off for school-based assessment and moderation except the prospect of a greater investment of time, resources and effort, teachers' commitment to their students leads them to favour student-centred rather than bureaucratic assessment. In particular in this project they favoured

> consensus moderation over inspection and statistical moderation because this implies that standards are constructed in social interaction, not drawn down to the humdrum reality of the moderation exercise from some ideal Platonic realm; and because the social negotiation model really does offer some pay-off for teachers in the form of participation, empowerment and professional development. It is likely to improve teaching and learning by developing awareness, raising self-respect and providing feedback via the teachers to the students . . . (standards) are thus socially negotiated, though in the real world where people and groups have different power ratification by representatives of society wider than those present at the moderation meetings is needed for acceptability to the users.
>
> (Shaw and Radnor, 1993, p. 249)

This quotation summarising the findings of a small regional certification initiative also summarises the findings of this international review. On the one hand it raises the key issue of credibility and the need, particularly in 'high-stakes' environments where much is at stake for the individual and/or the institution, for trustworthiness and transparency of the data in the interests of both efficiency and social justice. On the other, it raises the issue of professional development and the contribution of quality assurance and control arrangements to both individual and institutional development through appropriate feedback. Clearly differences in these two respects are likely to influence the complexity in character of the moderation methods used. National culture and tradition is likely to provide a further source of influence as it reflects public acceptability of different approaches. As Figure 2.1 sets out, the choice between more bureaucratic or more professional approaches to quality assurance and control, represents a 'trade-off' between different costs and benefits.

The lesson from this review, however, is that for such decisions to be made rationally rather than arbitrarily, there is an urgent need

(1) for international research evidence concerning the relative effectiveness of the full range of moderation approaches in terms of (a) consistency of standards, (b) professional development, (c) public credibility;

(2) for policy-makers to be challenged to identify their assessment priorities in these terms and to demonstrate how well the moderation procedures being employed meet these;

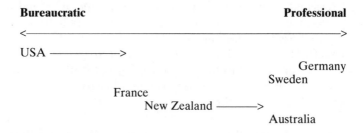

orientation:	norm-referenced	criteria-referenced
purpose:	selection	attestation of competence
priority:	reliability	validity/utility
techniques:	standardised	mixed, performance-based
status:	high	lower

Figure 2.1 Priorities and trends in six different countries' approach to providing for quality in assessment

(3) to explore in the light of national educational culture and assessment traditions, the most effective strategies for bringing about change in both professional practice and public attitudes.

Acknowledgements

I am greatly indebted to Dr Caroline Gipps and Professor Margaret Sutherland for some of the material in this chapter.

References

Australian Cooperative Assessment Programme *Newsletter* 1990, no. 2.

Baker, E. L., O'Neil, H. F. and Linn, R. L. (1991) Policy and validity prospects for performance-based assessment. Paper presented at the annual meeting of the American Psychological Association, August.

Baumgart, N. and McBryde, B. (1992) Admission to higher education: contrasts in two neighbouring Australian states. Paper presented to 18th Annual Conference of the IAEA, Dublin.

Berlak, H., Newmann, F. M., Adams, E., Archbald, D. A., Burgess, T., Raven, J. and Romberg, T. A. (eds) (1992) *Towards a New Science of Educational Testing and Assessment*, State University of New York, Albany.

Caroff, A. (1991) Evaluation et validation des acquis: le diplôme national du brevet, in *Ministère de L'Education, Rapport sur l'Envaluation des Acquis des Elèves à la Fin des Cycles d'Apprentissage*, Ministry of Education, Paris.

Crossley, M. and Broadfoot, P. (1992) Comparative and international research in education: scope, problems and potential, *British Educational Research Journal*, Vol. 18, no. 2, pp. 99–112.

Kreeft, H. P. J. (1990) *Examinations in Europe: Three Major Streams*, Paper presented to the annual conference of the International Association for Educational Assessment, Maastricht, Netherlands.

Linn, R. (1991) Technical considerations in the proposed nationwide assessment system for the national education goals panel. Prepared for the Technical Planning Sub Group of the Goal 3 Resource Group to the National Education Educational Goals Panel.

Madaus, G. (1993) A national testing system: manna from above? An historical/technological perspective, *Educational Assessment*, Vol. 1, no. 1, pp. 9–26.

Madaus, G. E. and Kellaghan, T. (1991) *Student Examination Systems in the EC: Lessons for the United States*, Washington DC Office of Technology Assessment.

National Commission on Excellence in Education (1983) *A Nation at Risk: the imperative for educational reform.* Washington, D.C.: U.S. Govermment Printing Office.

Neather, E. J. (1993) The Arbitur examination, *Language Learning Journal*, no. 7, March, pp. 19–21.

Nelson, D. (1993) Personal communication.

NZQA (New Zealand Qualifications Authority) (1991a) *Designing a Moderation System*, NZQA, Wellington, New Zealand.

NZQA (New Zealand Qualifications Authority) (1991b) *QA News*, Issue 10, November, NZQA, Wellington, New Zealand.

NZQA (New Zealand Qualifications Authority) (1992) *Moderation of Assessment: An Introduction for National Standards Bodies*, NZQA, Wellington, New Zealand.

Office of Technology Assessment, US Congress (1992) *Asking the Right Question: Testing in America*, Government Printing Office, Washington DC.

Phillips, D. (1989) Crossnational attractions in education, *Comparative Education*, Vol. 25, no. 3.

Phillips, D. (1989) 'Neither a borrower nor a lender be? The problems of cross-national attraction in education'. *Comparative Education*, Vol. 25, no. 3.

Prost Report (1983) *Les lycées et leurs études au seuil du xxle siecle: rapport du Groupe de Travail National sur les Seconds Cycles.* Preside par Antoine Prost. Publisher: Ministère de l'Education Nationale, Service Information.

Sadler, R. (1989) Formative assessment and the design of instructional systems, *Instructional Science*, Vol. 18, pp. 119–44.

Sadler, R. (1991) *Qualifications for the 21st century. Standards-based assessment in the secondary school: the Queensland experience* Wellington. N.Z.: New Zealand Qualifications Authority.

Shaw, K. E. and Radnor, H. (1993) Moderation in assessment: the case of MAP–SW, *Research Papers in Education*, Vol. 8, June, pp. 227–49.

Shepard, L. (1991) Psychometricians' beliefs about learning, *Educational Researcher*, Vol. 20, pp. 2–16.

SSABSA (Senior Secondary Assessment Board of South Australia) (1988) *Information Booklet No. 2 Assessment and Moderation*, SSABSA, South Australia.

Sutherland, M. (1993) Assessment in Germany, in J. Nisbett (ed.) *Assessment and Curriculum Reform*, OECD, Paris.

Sydney Morning Herald (1993) Editorial, 30 November, p. 12.

Tucker, M. and Resnick, L. B. (1990) Setting a new standard: toward an examination system for the United States. Proposal for the New Standards Project, University of Pittsburgh.

Viviani, N. (1990) *The Review of Tertiary Entrance in Queensland.* Report submitted to the Minister for Education, Brisbane.

Withers, G. (1992) Achieving comparability of school-based assessments used within tertiary admissions procedures – the Australian experience. Paper given at International Association for Educational Assessment, Dublin.

3

QUALITY IN EXTERNAL ASSESSMENT

David Satterly

The intention in this chapter is to take a close and critical look at external assessment, defined as assessment where the tasks are set by someone outside the school or college, even though the marking may be carried out by the teacher or lecturer. In doing this we are extending to external assessment the possibility of the same criticisms as are levelled at internal assessment. We address questions, in the light of research evidence, which challenge the traditional confidence in external assessment. Are external assessments more dependable than teachers' assessments? What happens when we look beyond the large-scale statistics which are used to report reliability but which ignore differences at the level of the individual arising from the structure of tests and the context of items? Do we have enough information on which to judge the validity of the results of external assessment?

External assessment takes many forms: whole examinations or components in GCSE, A-level, standardised tests and National Curriculum standard tasks and standard assessment tests (SATs). Many procedures are followed and a variety of instruments used; the literature which has examined their character and quality is extensive (e.g. Wood, 1991). Rigorous criteria for the evaluation of assessment have been presented, notably by a joint committee representing the American Educational Research Association (AERA) and two other bodies (1985). Not all criteria are equally appropriate for all types of assessment but their application suggests that no single method or instrument currently in use is immune to criticism.

Copyright © 1994, David Satterly

The central problem of assessment

Although assessment can be carried out in many ways, using different modes of presentation and response which yield a number of outcomes, all share at least one common feature: each is based on only a sample of the performance of interest from which the assessors and other users of the result wish to generalise to the invariably much larger domain which it is assumed to represent. For example, whenever a teacher, however reluctantly, administers a SAT or other type of test his or her interest extends beyond the features of the response itself to an inference about what the students' answers suggest of their grasp of knowledge, skill or understanding on which successful performance is assumed to depend. Since it is not feasible to assess a student on every relevant item or task which could be set, an assessor inevitably risks making a judgement from limited evidence.

Research in the psychology of assessment has consistently demonstrated that small changes in task presentation, in response mode, in the conditions under which assessment takes place, in the relations between assessor and assessed and within students on different occasions all have an effect on the performance. This finding has influenced some psychologists to extend their understanding of learning by changing their focus from the cognitive processes assumed to underlie performance to the study of the forms of social engagement in which the performance is situated (Lave and Wenger, 1991). Indeed, it is not always clear what can be inferred from a student's 'success' or 'failure'. Success cannot always be attributed to some underlying competence or ability nor failure to its absence (Wood, 1987). A great deal remains to be discovered about the features of tasks and assessment context which evoke a student's 'best' performance (Messick, 1984). As early as 1874, T. H. Huxley drew attention to the fact that being successful in an examination does not always depend solely upon the student's knowledge. In his address, as Rector of the University of Aberdeen, he said: '[students] work to pass, not to know; and outraged science takes her revenge. They do pass, and they don't know' (Bibby, 1959, p. 37).

The problem of what exactly can be inferred from a performance remains a central question for all assessment techniques. The interpretation of any score, grade or descriptor depends upon how far it can be generalised from the performance observed to other tasks in the domain, to other occasions and settings, or across independent observers. Generalisability of external assessments is very limited since controlled conditions and timed papers are about as unlike real life as you can get (Nuttall, 1987, p. 116); they also fail to represent pretty well every other context in which what has been learned can be demonstrated or applied.

Many inferences, however, continue to be drawn from external assessment. Given that it is undertaken for such a wide variety of purposes (some incompatible if not inimical) it would be difficult to devise an assessment which would simultaneously satisfy all parties concerned. Many have pointed out that assessment for school accountability is not easily reconciled with assessment for diagnosis of learning difficulty. (See, for example, Gipps *et al.*, 1993.) Under such competing requirements, the 'best' assessment possible (that is, which commands the support of all who have an interest) would resemble a well-known brand of pocket-knife: though bristling with devices, none of them performs as well as the specialist tool.

The persistence of external assessment

Although flawed, the persistence in Britain and the USA of external assessment and testing owes something to the belief that the information it provides is in some way more dependable and valid than corresponding internal assessment either in its comparability and accuracy or in terms of the inferences which can be drawn from it about the performance of students and schools. Such beliefs are well summarised in the statement by Kahn (1990):

> Subscription to external examinations is frequently justified on the grounds that they offer a trustworthy standard. It is believed that, with thousands of candidates in each subject, examination standards will show little variation over time and provide an objective measure of worth. Furthermore, an external examination is, at least in theory, immune to corrupt influence.
>
> (Kahn, 1990, p. 514)

Since Kahn was writing about attitudes held in Botswana towards the Cambridge Overseas School Certificate, this attribution of trustworthiness is not confined to Britain where, if the final two words were substituted by, say, 'teacher bias' or 'teacher differences', the statement would find considerable support. At first sight there appears to be some truth in the statement since, prior to the introduction of common National Curriculum criteria, teachers necessarily awarded marks and grades in isolation and one function of external assessment was to enlarge the conceptions of achievement by reducing emphasis on local norms. However, the relatively low take-up of Mode 3 examining in GCE and CSE (Smith, 1976) might well have been attributable to teachers' lack of confidence that they had a firm grip on what was assumed to be more absolute standards. Unfortunately (for the students) the more finely tuned the internal assessment to the content of the teaching the less likely it is that the learning will be tapped by the content of a common external examination and, there-fore, the greater the likelihood that it will 'disappear' during statistical adjustment to place disparate scores on the same scale (Wood, 1987). For this reason, the practice of statistical moderation using reference tests has fallen into disuse in the UK (see Chapter 1, p. 21) though it is still used elsewhere, for example in Australia.

Where the external and the internal co-exist within an assessment sys-tem, however, their status appears to differ. Arrangements in GCSE per-mit a balance between internal and external assessment but this varies from board to board and subject to subject. The greater trustworthiness of exter-nal assessment is, however, implied by the preference given to SAT results over teachers' assessment in those targets covered by the national tests (DfE, 1992, p. 4). Similarly, in Holland, Luijten (1988) has reported that internal assessments are judged to be more lenient and less rigorous than the external components. One might expect, therefore, that the assumed superiority of external assessment has consistently been demonstrated, yet this conclusion is not always borne out by the evidence available.

Two concepts have dominated discussion of assessment quality for at least sixty years: reliability and validity (see Chapter 1, p. 12). No test score or grade is of much value, even if the instrument is of high techni-cal quality, if the information it provides is irrelevant or unhelpful in achieving the purpose for which assessment was undertaken: that is, it is of low validity. At the same time, few would be advised to interpret a result if it was subject to too much error, if it were known to vary from occasion to occasion, test form to test form, or assessor to assessor: that is, it is of low reliability. Yet the standards for reliability and validity are often in tension in practice as assessors strive to produce instruments or devise settings in which a range of worthwhile objectives may be as-sessed (Buckle and Riding, 1988; Nuttall, 1987). Recent developments in assessment have tended to emphasise validity in their attempts to re-place paper-and-pencil tests, for example, by those which resemble more closely the performance domain to which it is desired to generalise the result. There are signs, however, that reliability studies have been neglected in the past ten years (Wood, 1991).

Issues of reliability and validity during test construction

Differences between norm- and criterion-referenced assessment

Most studies of reliability and validity have been driven by classical psychometric considerations. However, Carver (1974) has argued that psychometric tests differ from most worthwhile educational assessments in their purpose. Whereas the former stress high reliability of norm-referenced measurement (often of abilities) the latter are concerned with achievement (the quantity and quality of students' learning following teaching), diagnosis or the identification of stages reached in the mastery of objectives as assessed by criterion-referenced tests.

High reliability in a psychometric sense entails the construction of a test which discriminates well among students and does so with little measurement error. This can be achieved by pre-testing items and the construction of a test which samples across a range of topics or domains. A criterion- or competence-based assessment, however, if it is to yield estimates of the amount of measurement error present, would have to consist of a number of items which test a single objective or domain. In practice, with many statements of student attainment to be assessed, too few items per objective can be constructed to assess each with a satisfactory degree of dependability. Test constructors must, therefore, seek to demonstrate reliability in ways that are different from the measurement error approach of psychometrics.

The dilemma for constructors of criterion-referenced tests has already been described by Harlen (Chapter 1, p. 22). Precise criteria of performance, which can be used reliably by different assessors, turn out to be too numerous to be of much value and are at a distance from worthwhile educational aims; statements which express complex and 'high-level' learning goals, on the other hand, cannot be used uniformly by different assessors. To date, there have been no systematic reports of the extent of inter-assessor reliability using complex criteria and hence the extent of the generalisability of the assessments cannot be evaluated.

Analytic and synthetic aspects of assessment

To limit the remaining discussion it is necessary to distinguish analytic from synthetic aspects of assessments. This chapter will focus on the former which refer to the intrinsic properties of the score, grade or description. The latter concern the effects of making the assessment on the student, teacher and processes of learning. Critics vary in the relative emphasis they place on each of these considerations (Harnish and Mabry, 1993). There is tension here, too: few teachers would be likely to show enthusiasm for an assessment, however brilliant its technical properties, if its educational impact was judged to be deleterious. We may note at this point that the actual effects of external assessment on teaching and learning are not entirely clear but teacher testimony is commonly that they can be deleterious and lead to an overemphasis on the transmission of facts (Scarth and Hammersley, 1988).

Classification of items and test validity

The study of reliability and validity of external assessments has to be retrospective, though their foundations can be established during design and construction. In the better published tests, claiming to measure named psychological or educational constructs, there is – or should be – continuing feedback between intention and outcome as items are tested and construct validity is investigated. All items begin their lives as aspirations to assess the required attribute and some sort of assessment plan ('blueprint' or 'specification table') is prepared usually in the form of a grid in which contents or domains intersect with something which resembles psychological processes or levels in a taxonomy of objectives (such as Bloom's *Taxonomy*, 1956). Given that most educational domains are open or very large (Berk, 1980), almost any number of items per cell in the grid could be prepared. Examination boards, though building examinations from scratch each year, rely on experts and experience with previous papers to prepare items. An achievement test will, of course, be multidimensional in that a number of theoretically independent (or, at least, separately definable) dimensions are to be assessed. These may, nevertheless, be correlated in practice perhaps because of an unknown or hypothetical psychological 'glue' which binds them together (ability, motivation). One problem is how best to conceptualise these dimensions. Wood (1991) has pointed out that most boards seem to subscribe to one or other version of Bloom's taxonomy (he provides examples).

Any categorisation of items faces two problems in particular. Firstly, it is difficult to prepare 'pure' items which measure only one level × content intersection partly because an analytic scheme for the classification of objectives has been confused with a hierarchical theory of the structure of human ability. Secondly, a given item can be answered 'correctly' by different strategies or competences: student A might achieve a correct answer by recall whereas student B may gain the same credit by a process of reasoning or 'problem-solving'. Claims that items can be constructed to assess the different underlying competences which make up the global concept of achievement are often made. Wood (1991) provides examples from GCSE. But these, and similar claims, must be backed up by empirical evidence if their validity for these inferences is to be established. There are remarkably few studies of the construct validity of achievement tests and examinations, that is, whether tests actually measure what they claim to measure. Boards do not seem to see the publication of such details as a high priority. In its absence one must conclude that the classification of content is to demonstrate awareness of the need to sample as wide a range of levels of objectives as possible but not success in doing so.

Structure of assessments

The information provided about standardised published tests is of uneven quality (see, for example, Levy and Goldstein, 1984; Hall, 1985). Most manuals, however, do provide details of the selection and construction of items and the principles which guide their arrangement in the tests. The selection and arrangement of items in a test or examination has consequences for the reliability and validity and hence the meaning of scores or grades. The most important are:

(a) The spread of difficulty of items may be too small to enable the reliable differentiation of grades. The separation of highest from average grades has, in some cases, been made on very small raw score differences.

(b) Many papers or examinations contain a mixture of item types. This creates problems of the interpretation of scores which, though numerically equivalent, are qualitatively different.

(c) The performance of students can be affected by the sequence and difficulty gradient of items within test papers. Familiar examples include those where several questions are based upon a single stimulus and where response to later items is conditional upon earlier ones. If students are unsuccessful early in the assessment this can harm morale and affect their later performance.

(d) Estimates of item difficulty in external assessments are based either on the subjective judgements of examiners or on group-based facility indexes. These do not correspond with difficulty as perceived by individual students and experience has shown that minor rearrangements of context or the provision of cues can affect performance on logically equivalent items (Hodson, 1987).

(e) The trend towards greater use of differentiated papers (see below) creates problems of comparability analogous to those in point (b) above.

Information from those who prepare external examinations concerning the design of questions, item selection and sequencing is very sparse. Little appears to have changed in this respect in recent years (Willmott and Hall, 1975). These structural features do, however, directly affect the performance of students and the reliability and validity of the result. Quite clearly, external assessment is too inflexible to provide the best estimate of a student's performance. Use of a range of situations and a variety of methods, as in teacher assessment, is fairer to students and far more likely to yield a generalisable and informative outcome.

Control of quality and comparability

The aspects of quality control of external assessment which are likely to receive greatest attention are those required by the Education Act, 1988. The School Curriculum and Assessment Authority (SCAA) has been charged with the responsibility of keeping *all* (my emphasis) aspects of examination and assessment under review and to disseminate information relating to them. Recent publications (SEAC, 1992) give some indication of the principal focus. They have spoken of putting in place a number of measures to ensure quality, namely 'SEAC scrutinies, inter-Board comparability studies and various statistical comparisons carried out within the Boards'. Assessment users and students are also assured that 'OFSTED also carries out its own monitoring activity' (p. 1) but those interested in examination quality will be disappointed to note that the third publication (of 'information relating to examinations and assessment') consists only of tables which present the percentages of candidates gaining the grades in various subjects.

The study of inter-board comparability is basically of the extent to which standards 'remain the same' across boards and subjects. The literature suggests that this has been a major research interest which far exceeds the effort made in establishing construct validity of examinations. The belief is widely held by teachers that some boards are 'easier' than others but comparability is not easily established (Tattersall, 1983). Bardell, Forrest and Shoesmith (1985), Johnson and Cohen (1983) and Forrest and Shoesmith (1985) have indicated the many ways in which examination boards' results are equated with one another; the most meaningful type of comparison would be of students who take the 'same' examination set by different boards (though it is not clear why they should be equivalent if content is differently sampled and construct validity unknown). The number of such candidates is small and, where papers are exchanged and marked, too small for much to be learnt.

The variation between boards has recently been examined by Tymms and FitzGibbon (1991). Their study suggests that teachers have overestimated its extent. At A-level at least the assumption that some boards are consistently more lenient than others receives little support. Some variation is, of course, consistent with differences in the populations taking the examinations across boards and within subjects from year to year (Glas, 1988). If facility values are known there is a greater likelihood that comparable tests can be prepared but where item types differ 'new' papers are unlikely to be of the same difficulty as 'old'. Comparability is usually assumed to demonstrate uniformity of grading standards but it is ensured by statistical scaling not by comparable content or examining methods. High comparability is consistent with the public's belief that if a given student took, say, mathematics set by two or more boards (s)he would be expected to gain the same grade in each. But it is not very meaningful to assert that if (s)he obtained A for maths but B for French (s)he is 'better' at one than the other. So long as an overall grade can be obtained by a differentially weighted mixture of papers, comparing performance or quantifying learning (as distinct from tabulating percentages gaining grades) is hazardous. It remains to be seen whether the inter-board comparability studies promised by SCAA will provide external examination users with more information about this aspect of quality than at present.

Reliability

Although it is quite common to hear talk (even by experts) of 'test reliability', this can be misleading since it is the score or grade awarded that is subject to error, not the test or examination. Reliability coefficients vary from sample to sample and with the method of estimation employed, but the purpose of reliability study is to calculate an estimate for the standard error of measurement which enables the score user to quantify the uncertainty associated with it and to estimate the limits around obtained scores within which true scores lie. If the scores are chunked to provide grades then the accuracy of the result can never be less than plus or minus one grade. If one is interested in the reliability of marks awarded by different assessors, say for essays, then it is permissible to think of the true score for the essay as the mean mark or grade awarded by a number of qualified assessors and reliability the correlation between pairs of markers. If assessors are not required to provide marks but to decide whether or not a student's work shows evidence of criterion behaviour or statement of attainment ('ticking boxes') in the National Curriculum, something analogous to an estimate of reliability can be obtained by calculating the percentage of perfect agreement between independent assessors across the sample of students under scrutiny. The method of estimating reliability preferred by statisticians is to correlate at least two equivalent assessments. The one-off nature of almost all external assessment precludes this, of course.

All these methods of reliability estimation are intended to qualify the variation in assessment which occurs across the limited number of sources of error which are taken into account. Modern methods of reliability study often combine identifiable sources of variance into a single index of generalisability but the separate components of variance show where sources of error lie. Such studies must be carefully designed but, even then, sources of error can be confounded (Lehmann, 1990). The overall aim of studies is to identify where and how much error resides in test score grades or assessors' ratings and, therefore, whether the result can be depended upon.

Problems of the dependability of scores and grades occur where papers are marked by many assessors. Boards apparently take considerable care to minimise this potential source of error. Moderation, discussion and standardisation of draft marking schemes, agreement of schemes, cross-validation of trial scripts, a common code of practice to be maintained throughout the marking, checks during the marking period and later adjustments, if necessary, have been features of external assessment for many years. Nevertheless, where subjectivity plays a part, marks or grades will inevitably differ between assessors, within an assessor on different occasions and, for the student, between topics if more than one is set, even where the same construct is supposedly assessed. High correlations between two or more assessors and between scores conducted on two or more topics are not always obtained in the marking of written work. An early study by Hartog and Rhodes (1936) demonstrated this quite clearly and little had changed by the time of the enquiries by Britton, Martin and Rosen (1966) and by Hewitt (1967). The latter found that correlations between two English papers, averaging at about 0.60, where no greater than that between papers in English and French (coefficients ranged from 0.79 in one school sample to 0.21 in another). In fact, the correlations between the two English papers were no higher than between either paper and teachers' internal estimates. Of particular interest was Hewitt's conclusion that 'awards' based on internal assessments, moderated externally, appear to be no less reliable than the traditional External Examination' (p. 26). When dealing with the reliability of a two-and-a-half-hour paper taken by more than 2,400 candidates drawn from twenty-three schools, Hewitt found that the error was such that the average student had a one-in-three chance of rising or falling by as much as four grades.

The 1970s saw an increase in the number of reliability studies (Nuttall and Willmott, 1972; Willmott and Nuttall, 1975; Willmott and Hall, 1975). During the course of these surveys a number of external examinations was studied and reliability coefficients in some cases were quite high. Willmott and Nuttall, for example, found coefficients to range from about 0.7 to 0.9 for nearly thirty examination papers studied. More recently, Murphy (1978, 1982) confirmed the finding that coefficients were lowest for mark–re-mark reliabilities of written work.

Such difficulties persist, as Lehmann (1990) has shown. In an enquiry designed to investigate four sources of variance (between and within assessors, between topics and within students), Lehmann concluded that the measurement of writing achievement was 'not very good'. Of particular interest to the present discussion – and to the detriment of the views of those who believe that external assessment of written work based on one or two topics is accurate – is the conclusion that a minimum of thirteen written assigmnents would be required to attain a satisfactory coefficient of generalisability. In spite of the application of clear criteria for assessment almost 12 per cent of the variance in final scores could be attributed to differences between and within assessors. Inter-assessor agreement is itself known to vary with the topic and length of the written work (Wesdorp, Bauer and Purves, 1982) but by far the greatest source of variation comes from the interaction of student with task. This suggests a serious limitation on the reliability of assessments of written work even in the 'best' external examination where only few – and, for some candidates, uninteresting – topics can be set. Teacher assessment over time and task is, potentially, better equipped to overcome this drawback and to reach a dependable conclusion about the worth of students' written work.

Although some of the reliabilities found in studies now more than ten years old are as high as could reasonably be expected, one cannot assume – in the absence of information to the contrary issued by examination boards – that they have been maintained, especially in the far more complex types of differentiated examination paper currently in use. If reliabilities were reported and margins of error attached to the scores or grades they would, if large, be a source of embarrassment to those who otherwise take on trust a published result. It seems inevitable, given some of the above difficulties and the lack of fashion for reliability studies, that the dependability of scores and grades in many external forms of assessment will continue to be unknown to users and students alike.

Problems of establishing reliability in the new forms of external assessment have not yet been seriously engaged by production teams. Indeed, general interest has shifted from reliability to validity and towards criterion-referenced testing, the recognition of 'positive achievement', and assessments with formative and diagnostic properties. Some of those constructed not only involve many parts and modes of testing but also lean towards greater use of differentiated papers with the worthy aim of giving candidates across the full ability range the opportunity to demonstrate what they can do. Expanding the scope of assessment to the entire ability range can, in principle, add to reliability if all candidates take a common paper. Here, grade boundaries can be set with greater reliability since the spread of obtained scores is likely to be large. Differentiated papers present special problems. These papers are aimed at segments of the ability range and usually follow one of three principal models (Gipps and Stobart, 1993). In keeping with aims of GCSE to emphasise positive achievement, candidates enter at the level where they can expect a reasonable chance of success but, at the same time, the papers must discriminate between candidates at the ability level which is necessarily restricted. Problems in setting papers of different difficulty levels (however 'difficulty' is operationalised) which, at the same time, are reliable enough to set grade limits are likely to prove complex (Stobart, 1987).

One relevant enquiry has been published by Good and Cresswell (1988). Using examination papers in history and physics which figured common, alternative and extension papers, the authors concluded that greatest errors occurred in the application of grade boundaries on components of different difficulty. Use of 'stored mental models' of grades in previous years was found to be an inadequate basis for judgement and candidates – had they known – would have been well advised to enter at the lower level of a differentiated examination since assessors judged performance to be higher in 'easy' than in 'hard' components. This is clearly unsatisfactory and the common scale appears elusive. Moreover, problems in choosing the appropriate level at which a student should enter are proving difficult to solve (IGRC, 1992).

It seems clear that the problems in reliability testing are not diminished by changes in the structure of contemporary British external assessment. Given the use of external results as a means of comparing schools' performance the need for reliable indicators of achievement which are also valid for this purpose is enhanced. It is time for the legal insistence on publication of school examination results to be matched by similar openness about reliability in the great body of external assessment on which these comparisons rest.

Validity

Questions of validity are at the core of recent developments in assessment. The purpose of validation is to establish what inferences can correctly be drawn from the result of the assessment whether score, grade or descriptor applied.

Content validity

Content validity is of particular importance in National Curriculum tests and tests of achievement. It is established by a demonstration that the items in the test or examination represent the domains which it is desired to measure. In the case of SATs this entails that the items assess performance against attainment targets, not only in their subject matter but also in the intellectual processes involved. Content validity can be built into a test if the selection of items is judged by experts to sample the area of knowledge, skill or understanding which constitutes the objectives of teaching and learning. In a National Curriculum test it should be clear what a given item is designed to test though this is not subject to negotiation with teachers, as has already been pointed out in Chapter 1 (p. 22). The construction of an external examination or achievement test is aided by a specification table where named topics intersect with processes and which indicates which topic on a syllabus or aspect of teaching each item is ostensibly to assess. In the case of achievement tests the relative balance of different items should reflect their emphasis in the course of study.

It is clear that external assessments designed to be taken by a large number of students cannot be finely tuned to the learning experiences in classrooms and, as such, can have only limited content validity for the courses and variety of learning styles which exist. The information they provide as to just how well a student has achieved is, therefore, limited. Most external testing agencies do not provide a detailed description of the knowledge, skill or understanding being assessed nor how items have been sampled to represent the domains. As Thorndike (1982) has pointed out;

> test evaluators have generally been satisfied with making a subjective and qualitative estimation of the congruence between curricular objectives and test content and expressing their evaluation in narrative form. . . . So there is not a great deal to be said about a theory or a methodology for evaluating content validity.
>
> (Thorndike, 1982, p. 185)

Construct validity

Few assessments are undertaken merely to document the features of a student's performance ('*x* has solved the equations on this occasion') but to draw conclusions about the student's underlying competence ('*x* has the ability to solve this type of equation'). In the latter case an inference has been drawn from the performance about the theoretical explanation of the individual differences observed (the construct of 'ability' in this example). Thus, the construct validity of a test is the extent to which it assesses the underlying concept which it claims to measure. Educational assessment is not always concerned with the measurement of constructs but, as Wood (1991) has pointed out, there are many instances where constructs have been invoked in score interpretation. Mathematics items, for example, are sometimes said to make separate assessment of constructs such as 'understanding' and 'interpretation' (Ridgway, 1988). If claims are made that tests or subsets of items can differentiate under-lying constructs they must be supported by evidence that this has been achieved in practice.

Evidence of construct-related validity of external educational tests is, however, extremely sparse but, in its absence, one cannot be confident as to just which (desirable) competences are being assessed by them. Lack of construct validation lends spurious support to the making of many familiar statements, such as 'This is just measuring memory' or 'Worthwhile educational objectives cannot be assessed', though it is not always clear what is being asserted by either. As methods of assessment in education have become more varied and their targets widened to include higher-level thinking skills the need for construct validation studies is enhanced. It is conceivable, of course, that competencies re-quired for effective functioning at high levels in a society of increasing complexity and flux cannot be assessed in the artificial and formal set-tings so typical of schools. Although paper-and-pencil tests and exam-inations are 'unlike real life', the extension of this argument invokes questions of the transferability of school learning to the ever increasing complexity of modern existence which it would be unwise to enter here!

The few empirical studies of the validity of external assessments that have been carried out have been criterion related, not least because they are the easiest type of validation to carry out (Wood, 1987). To validate an assessment in this way entails a study of the relationship of scores, grades or descriptors to an independent criterion, either assessed con-currently or in the future. Unwittingly, perhaps, teachers have been arguing the concurrent validity of National Curriculum tests (SATS) at ages seven and eleven by saying that the information they provide dupli-cates what teachers already know from their own assessments about the features of pupils' performance and their relative standing in relation to the attainment of objectives. Concurrent validity is unexciting to test users because, if demonstrated, it shows that one test duplicates another in the information it provides.

Although it is common to hear of other aspects of the validity of assessments (in motivating pupils, in improving or focusing the pro-cesses of learning and teaching, and so on) these, though important, are not questions of the validity of the inference drawn from scores, grades and the like. Since they are, in essence, questions about the impact of methods of assessment and not validity of the assessment (that is, they are synthetic considerations) they will not be examined here.

Conclusion

Harlen (Chapter 1) has proposed that quality in assessment entails four features:

(1) It should be valid: that is, it should assess those aspects of students which it claims to assess.
(2) It should be as reliable as possible given the limitations imposed by the search for high validity.
(3) It should provide information suited to the purpose for which it was undertaken.
(4) It should make demands on teachers and students compatible with the context in which learning is exhibited. This means that it should not be artificial, too time consuming, nor divorced from the normal range of contexts in which the educational achievements of students can be observed.

In the light of these criteria and the amount of information provided by external agencies, such as examination boards, the degree of trust placed in external examinations described in the opening sections of this chapter seems misplaced. The highly controlled and unrepresentative conditions under which much external assessment is made place serious limitations on the generalisability and validity of scores or grades. The inferences which can be drawn about students' performance in more meaningful contexts are, therefore, weak. Very little information is made available as to what is being assessed by external examinations. The claims by boards that different papers, sections of papers or individual items are assessing named competences are unsubstantiated by evidence. In other words, construct validity studies are seldom undertaken or reported.

The structure of external papers lacks the flexibility to allow students to show what they have learnt in a variety of ways and to best advantage. Policies and practice for item trial and selection and for dealing with the sequencing of difficulty within tests or examination papers are rarely, if ever, stated. Alternative response modes to given problems are seldom allowed. The conditions of external assessment inevitably differ from the circumstances under which the relevant learning took place and from those under which it was exercised and might subsequently be applied. Content validity of external assessment is probably highest for those students whose teacher has adhered closely to the syllabus.

Data on reliability of external examinations made available to users are thin. Although coefficients of reliability are routinely calculated for certain assessments, these are not always of the most appropriate type. However, it is not possible at the point of consumption to quantify the error inherent in the score or grade awarded. The amount of variation across different assessors where subjective judgements are made is not stated. In these important aspects of quality, information is sparse, scattered and unsatisfactory.

External examinations can provide only limited information of use to teachers. The purposes for which teachers assess are very different from those who look for certification and curriculum control (see Chapter 4). Thus, the impact of external assessment on the teachers' day-to-day decisions about teaching and learning seems minimal. National Curriculum testing is, in some respects, a little closer to teachers' concerns: the majority of these tests are criterion referenced but it is too early to appraise the quality they might eventually exhibit.

References

AERA (American Educational Research Association), American Psychological Association and National Council on Measurement in Education (1985) *Standards for Educational and Psychological Testing*, APA, Washington.

Bardell, G. S., Forrest, G. M. and Shoesmith, D. J. (1985) *Comparability in GCE Review of the Boards' Studies, 196477*, JMB on behalf of the GCE Examining Boards, Manchester.

Berk, R. A. (1980) *Criterion Referenced Measurement*, Johns Hopkins University Press, Baltimore.

Bibby, C. (1959) *T. H. Huxley: Scientist, Humanist and Educator*, Watts, London.

Bloom, B. S. *et al.* (1956) *Taxonomy of Educational Objectives, Handbook I: Cognitive Domain*, Longman, London.

Britton, J. N., Martin, N. C. and Rosen, H. (1966) *Multiple Marking of Comprehensions: An Account of an Experiment*, HMSO, London.

Buckle, C. F. and Riding, R. J. (1988) Current problems in assessment – some reflections, *Educational Psychology*, Vol. 8, pp. 299–306.

Carver, R. C. (1974) Two dimensions of tests: psychometric and edumetric, *American Psychologist*, Vol. 29, pp. 512–18.

DfE (Department for Education) (1992) *Testing 14-year-olds in 1992: Results of the National Curriculum Assessments in England*, DfE, London.

Forrest, G. M. and Shoesmith, D. J. (1985) *A Second Review of GCE Comparability Studies*, JMB on behalf of the GCE Examining Boards, Manchester.

Gipps, C., Broadfoot, P., Dockrell, B., Harlen, W. and Nuttall, D.L. (1992) Problems in national assessment: a research critique, in *Policy Issues in National Assessment*, BERA Dialogues 7, Multilingual Matters, London.

Gipps, C. and Stobart, G. (1993) *Assessment: A Teachers' Guide to the Issues* (2nd edn), Hodder & Stoughton, London.

Glas, C. A. W. (1988) Psychometric aspects of maintaining standards of examinations, *Educational Psychology*, Vol. 8, pp. 257–70.

Good, F. J. and Cresswell, M. (1988) Grade-awarding in differentiated examinations, *British Educational Research Journal*, Vol. 14, pp. 263–81.

Hall, B. W. (1985) Survey of the technical characteristics of published educational achievement tests, *Educational Measurement: Issues and Practice*, Vol. 4, pp. 6–14.

Harnish, D. L. and Mabry, L. (1993) Issues in the development and evaluation of alternative assessments, *Journal of Curriculum Studies*, Vol. 25, pp. 179–87.

Hartog, P. and Rhodes, E. C. (1936) *The Marks of Examiners*, Macmillan, London.

Hewitt, E. A. (1967) *The Reliability of GCE O-Level Examinations in English Language*, Occasional Publications, No. 27, JMB, Manchester.

Hodson, D. (1987) How important is question sequence? *Education in Chemistry*, Vol. 24, pp. 11–12.

IGRC (1992) *Differentiation in GCSE Mathematics Centres' Entry Decision-Making Policy*, Cambridge Local Examinations Syndicate.

Johnson, S. and Cohen, L. (1983) *Investigating Grade Comparability through Cross-Moderation*, Schools Council, London.

Kahn, M. J. (1990) Some questions concerning the standards of external examinations, *Studies in Educational Evaluation*, Vol. 16, pp. 513–27.

Lave, J. and Wenger, E. (1991) *Situated Learning: Legitimate Peripheral Participation*, Cambridge University Press.

Lehmann, R. H. (1990) Reliability and generalizability of ratings of compositions, *Studies in Educational Evaluation*, Vol. 16, pp. 501–12.

Levy, P. and Goldstein, H. (1984) *Tests in Education: A Book of Reviews*, Academic Press, London.

Luijten, A. J. M. (1988) Internal vs external assessment in the Dutch examinations at 16+ and 18+, *Educational Psychology*, Vol. 8, pp. 237–46.

Messick, S. (1984) The psychology of educational measurement, *Journal of Educational Measurement*, Vol. 21, pp. 215–38.

Murphy, R. J. L. (1978) Reliability of marking in eight GCE examinations, *British Journal of Educational Psychology*, Vol. 48, pp. 196–200.

Murphy, R. J. L. (1982) A further report of investigations into the reliability of marking of GCE examinations, *British Journal of Educational Psychology*, Vol. 52, pp. 58–63.

Nuttall, D. L. (1987) The validity of assessments, *European Journal of Psychology of Education*, Vol. 2, pp. 109–18.

Nuttall, D. L. and Willmott, A. S. (1972) *British Examinations: Techniques of Analysis*, NFER, Slough.

Ridgway, J. (1988) *Assessing Mathematical Attainment*, NFER, Windsor.

Scarth, J. and Hammersley, M. (1988) Examinations and testing: an exploratory study, *British Educational Research Journal*, Vol. 14, pp. 231–43.

SEAC (Schools Examination and Assessment Council) *A and AS Examinations: Results 1992*, HMSO, London.

Smith, C. H. (1976) *Mode III Examinations in the CSE and GCE: A Survey of Current Practice*, Schools Council Examinations Bulletin 34, Evans/Methuen Educational, London.

Stobart, G. (1987) Differentiation: a review of LEAG research. Unpublished paper, ULSEB.

Tattersall, K. (1983) *Differentiated Examinations: A Strategy for Assessment at 16+?* Schools Council Examinations Bulletin 42, Methuen, London.

Thorndike, R. L. (1982) *Applied Psychometrics*, Houghton Mifflin, Boston.

Tymms, P. B. and FitzGibbon, C. T. (1991) A comparison of examination boards: 'A'-levels, *Oxford Review of Education*, Vol. 17, pp. 17–32.

Wesdorp, H., Bauer, B. A. and Purves, A. C. (1982) Towards conceptualization of the scoring of written composition, *Evaluation in Education*, Vol. 5, pp. 299–315.

Willmott, A. S. and Hall, C. G. W. (1975) *'O'-Level Examined: The Effects of Question Choice*, Schools Council, London.

Willmott, A. S. and Nuttall, D. L. (1975) *The Reliability of Examinations at 16+*, Macmillan, London.

Wood, R. (1987) *Measurement and Assessment in Education and Psychology*, Falmer Press, London.

Wood, R. (1991) *Assessment and Testing: A Survey of Research*, Cambridge University Press.

4

QUALITY IN TEACHER ASSESSMENT

Caroline Gipps

Introduction

Assessments which teachers make of pupils' attainment and performance are called variously teacher assessment (although in the USA this refers to assessment of teachers), school-based assessment and formative assessment. Formative assessment is best viewed as a subset of teacher assessment while teacher assessment itself can be summative as well as formative.

Teacher assessment is essentially an informal activity: the teacher may pose questions, observe activities, evaluate pupils' work in a planned and systematic or *ad hoc* way. The information which the teacher thus obtains may then be partial or fragmentary; it will not at the time allow the teacher to make a firm evaluation of the pupils' competence in reading, for example, or understanding of a mathematical process. But repeated assessment of this sort, over a period of time, and in a range of contexts *will* allow the teacher to build up a solid and broadly based understanding of the pupil's attainment. Because of these characteristics teacher assessment may be seen as having high validity (see Chapter 1). If the teacher assessment is used for formative purposes which then results in improved learning then the assessment can be said to have consequential validity, that is, it has the consequences expected/required of it. If the assessment has sampled broadly across the domain *and* in depth within it then the assessment is likely to be generalisable (within

Copyright © 1994, Caroline Gipps

that domain), since the teacher's evaluation of the pupil's ability to read at a certain level or to be able to manipulate single digits, will be based on a broad sample of tasks and assessments. An external test, on the other hand, will provide more limited information based as it is on a one-off occasion covering a limited sample of tasks.

Formative assessment

Formative assessment involves using assessment information to feed back into the teaching/learning process; some believe that assessment is only truly formative if it involves the pupil, others that it *can* be a process which involves only the teacher who feeds back into curriculum planning. The rationale of formative assessment is linked with the constructivist model of learning. In this model it is important to understand what the child knows and how she articulates it in order to develop her knowledge and understanding. In this model it is learning with understanding which counts and to this end information about existing ideas and skills is essential. Work in psychology and learning tells us similarly that for effective learning the task must be matched to the child's current level of understanding (Gipps, 1992a) and either pitched at that level to provide practice or slightly higher in order to extend and develop the child's skills. If the new task is much too easy the child can become bored, if much too difficult the child can become demotivated. Assessment to find out what and how children know is thus part of good teaching practice and in helping the teacher to decide what and how to teach next is formative assessment. However, if it is to be really fruitful it seems that the pupil must also be involved, since teachers need to explain to pupils what they need to do to improve their work or the next steps in the learning process.

Sadler (1989) conceptualises formative assessment as being concerned with how judgements about the quality of students' responses can be used to shape and improve their competence by short-circuiting the randomness and inefficiency of trial-and-error learning. The key difference between formative assessment and summative assessment is not timing, but purpose and effect: assessments made *during* the course of a unit or session may be used for summative or grading purposes rather than for truly formative purposes.

In Sadler's classic paper formative assessment is connected with feedback and for him feedback to teacher and pupil are separated: 'Teachers use feedback to make programmatic decisions with respect to readiness, diagnosis and remediation. Students use it to monitor the strengths and weaknesses of their performances, so that aspects associated with success or high quality can be recognised and reinforced, and unsatisfactory aspects modified or improved' (Sadler, 1989, p. 120). Sadler's work in theorising formative assessment stems from the 'common but puzzling' observation that even when teachers give students valid and reliable judgements about their work improvement does not necessarily follow. In order for the student to improve s/he must have: a notion of the desired standard or goal, be able to compare the actual performance with the desired performance and to engage in appropriate action to close the gap between the two. Feedback from the teacher, which helps the student with the second of these stages, needs to be of the kind and detail which tells the student what to do to improve; the use of grades or 'good, 7/10' marking cannot do this. Grades may in fact shift attention away from the criteria and be counterproductive for formative purposes. In Sadler's model, grades do not count as feedback: information fed back to the student is only feedback when it can be used to close the gap.

A key aspect of formative assessment, and an indispensable condition for improvement, is that the student comes to hold a notion of the standard or desired quality similar to that of the teacher, is able to monitor the quality of what is being produced at the time of production, and is able to regulate their work appropriately.

When the student reaches this stage the process is referred to as self-monitoring (rather than feedback from the teacher). Competent learners are those who self-monitor their work, although this does not mean that the need for feedback from the teacher decreases: such feedback will continue to be necessary whenever a new subject, standard or criterion is introduced.

Teacher assessment in practice

In our ESRC-funded study of teachers' assessment practice at primary school level, we spent a considerable amount of time trying to understand how teachers made their assessments for the teacher assessment (TA) element of national assessment (McCallum *et al.*, 1993). While infants' teachers had, prior to the introduction of national assessment, made informal assessments in the basic skills in order to write holistic descriptions of pupil progress for parents, assessing in relation to tightly specified criteria at different levels was a completely new requirement. Most of the resources for the development of national assessment went into producing test materials with little support for teacher assessment or training. Given that teachers had little preparation or support by way of a model for TA, it was not surprising that we found they adopted a range of procedures.

Models of teacher assessment

We grouped teachers' approaches into three models called Intuitives, Evidence Gatherers and Systematic Planners. These models, though describing teachers' practice in assessment, link in with teachers' (implicit) views of learning; they also link with different attitudes and approaches to criterion-referenced assessment and formative assessment.

The Intuitives rely on their memory in making and recording assessment so that there is a lack of observable TA. They do not refer to statements of attainment, they do not take notes, they reject systematic recorded assessment as too formal and structured an approach. Their assessment style is essentially intuitive: only the teacher can assess the child, assessment is built on close, all-round knowledge of children. This group of teachers could be broken down into two subgroups. The first, the Children's Needs Ideologists, have an exploratory or 'scaffolded' view of learning, in which they provide a stimulating environment and guide children towards discovering or learning. The second subgroup, the Tried and Tested Methodologists, have a more didactic model of teaching and learning: they see assessment as assessing what is taught. Both subgroups resist criterion-referenced assessment, that is assessment in relation to statements of attainment: the Children's Needs Ideologists because it is in tension with the 'whole child' philosophy, the Tried and Tested Methodologists because it means a radical change in behaviour for them. These teachers continued to incorporate children's effort or performance in relation to their background factors when making an assessment; their resistance to criterion-referenced approaches is epitomised by their reluctance to internalise or to have readily available the statements of attainment.

As for the formative nature of teacher assessment, the Tried and Tested Methodologists were essentially summative: they would sit down at the end of a term or half-term and 'call up their memory' and record an assessment for each child in relation to each attainment target. The Children's Needs Ideologists would say that they were constantly making formative assessments, but they could not articulate this, neither was it visible. In carrying out their essentially summative assessments, both of these subgroups made use of assessment procedures with which they were familiar, such as the ILEA Check Points, their own or school-developed worksheets and tests and mathematics worksheets from published schemes. This is in spite of the fact that the results from these did not relate to the levels and attainment targets of the National Curriculum.

The Evidence Gatherers collect evidence, written or drawn, in order to have a basis for making assessments. Some of these teachers collected hordes of evidence. At the end of each term or half-term, they would sit down and go through all the evidence and assign levels: this group does not rely on memory, since they feel that they need more than that to make an accurate assessment. However, often there is too much evidence to be used, and the teachers do not interrogate it all; part of the reason for collecting so much evidence seems to be that the evidence proves that the National Curriculum has been covered. In addition, collecting evidence in this way does not interfere with their normal teaching and classroom practice. These teachers tend to plan their work using the broad attainment targets and wait for assessment opportunities to arise rather than planning for assessment. The model of learning held by these teachers is essentially a traditional, didactic model: children learn what is taught and only what is taught; assessment follows teaching to check that the process is going according to plan. These teachers' view of criterion-referenced assessment is interesting in that they understand the idea of assessment in relation to criteria, but insist that context and pupil's background must sometimes be taken into account in judging performance; again they do not use statements of attainment. For this group of teachers, teacher assessment is essentially summative; however, this group is becoming aware of a range of assessment procedures and recognised the importance of observation, and of children's talk, in making informal assessments.

Both the Evidence Gatherers and the Intuitives, rather than using statements of attainment, tended to have an overall notion of 'levelness' and therefore seemed to rely on implicit norms in judging children's performance. Some of the teachers, because of the quasi norm-referenced use of levels, tended to use Level 3 to indicate children of well above average attainment. Thus they ridiculed the possibility that children might, at this age, be reaching Level 4. Our observations, however, indicated that in some of the schools (and not always those in affluent areas) pupils were indeed able to achieve Level 4 in some parts of the curriculum.

Systematic Planners plan specifically for teacher assessment: they identify activities and tasks within their planned programme of teaching with specific statements of attainment in mind. They use multiple techniques for assessment: observation, open-ended questioning, teacher/ pupil discussion, running records, scrutiny of written work. There are two subgroups which we call Systematic Assessors and Systematic Integrators. The Systematic Assessors give daily, concentrated time to assessment and separate themselves off from the rest of the class to do it. For the Systematic Integrators, assessment is integrated with regular classroom work and often the teacher circulates through the class gathering her evidence in different ways. These teachers have a constructivist approach to learning: children learn in idiosyncratic ways and not always what is taught. They also have a particular view about assessment, which means that they are keen to arrive at shared meanings in relation to grading children's work with colleagues. Teachers in this group understand and operate a criterion-referenced model of assessment. They use statements of attainment openly and regularly, often broken down into more detailed 'can-do' lists. Information about effort, progress and performance in relation to background go into records of achievement or children's personal records.

The significant difference between this group and the other two is their use of statements of attainment. These teachers also seem to be carrying out formative assessment in that assessment feeds into their planning on a regular and systematic basis, the children's records are accessible and used (something which we did not see with the other two groups) and they see real value in continuous, formative assessment as enhancing their professional development and effectiveness as teachers. This group of teachers do not necessarily maintain a model of formative assessment which involves making goals clear to the child, feeding back information directly related to those goals to the child, discussing and setting standards with the child and attempting to make them self-monitoring learners. In fact, this sort of feedback, in relation to specific assessment criteria, was almost never observed in the Key Stage 1 classes where we worked and it may be that this model is more appropriate to older pupils.

With no model of TA offered to teachers, it is perhaps not surprising that they came up with a range of approaches. These approaches were related to the teachers' views of teaching and learning, their general style of organisation and teaching, and their reaction to the imposition of National Curriculum assessment. They were thus developing assessment practice in line with their general practice and philosophy of primary education. What is important though, for ensuring quality in teacher assessment, is that teachers should relate their assessment to the given criteria, or exemplars, and that they be encouraged to discuss the levels which they award to particular pieces of work and/or children. We believe that these models are helpful in allowing us to see where primary teachers may be in their views about assessment in relation to the use of criteria and exemplars, since we see these as key issues for ensuring quality in teacher assessment, particularly where it is to be used for reporting purposes.

Reliability and validity in teacher assessment

A highly reliable test is of little use if it is not valid – but a test cannot be valid, in classical test theory, if it does not have a basic level of reliability.

Although texts on educational measurement tend to maintain that validity is more important than reliability, in fact developments in psychological and standardised testing have emphasised reliability. In the attempt to achieve highly accurate and replicable testing, the validity of the tests has often been neglected. The move towards performance-based assessment and the development of school-based teacher assessment are part of an attempt to redress the balance between reliability and validity. What is needed, is, of course, an appropriate balance between the two because they are in tension; Harlen's chapter argues this very cogently and puts forward our concept of quality in assessment, which derives from optimising validity *and* reliability.

In considering the traditional requirements for reliability and validity, Sadler suggests that, in view of the purpose of formative assessment, we reverse the polarity of the terms. In summative assessment reliability is presented

> as a precondition for a consideration of validity. In discussing formative assessment, however, the relation between reliability and validity is more appropriately stated as follows: validity is a sufficient but not necessary condition for reliability. Attention to the validity of judgements about individual pieces of work should take precedence over attention to reliability of grading in any context where the emphasis is on diagnosis and improvement. *Reliability will follow as a corollary.*
>
> (Sadler, 1989, p. 122, emphasis added)

The requirement that students improve as a result of feedback can be seen as a consequential validity criterion for formative assessment. In this model the teacher must involve the student in discussion of the evaluation and what is needed to improve, otherwise the student is unlikely to be able to improve her or his work; furthermore the student needs to be involved in this process in order to shift to a process of self-monitoring. Formative assessment thus needs to demonstrate formative validity and in Sadler's definition *must* involve feedback to the pupil; her or his involvement in and understanding of this feedback is crucial otherwise improvement is unlikely to occur.

We need to consider here the issue of purpose (and fitness for purpose). If teacher assessment is to be used for certification or accountability then it needs an adequate level of reliability, in terms of consistency of performance and scoring, for comparability purposes. If, however, the assessment is to be used for formative purposes, validity (content, construct *and* consequential aspects) is highly important and reliability is less so. Where school-based teacher assessment is concerned confusion often arises since reliability may be thought to be less important in a generic sense. However, this ignores the interaction with purpose: if teacher assessment is part of an accountability or certificating process, then reliability is important. The key, as Harlen makes clear, is how to achieve optimum reliability for the assessment's purpose while maintaining high validity.

Various methods of moderation together with training and the setting of criteria for grading are capable of enhancing reliability in teacher assessment. Mislevy suggests that moderation should be viewed as a way to specify the rules of the game, 'It can yield an agreed-upon way of comparing students who differ quantitatively, but it doesn't make information from tests that aren't built to measure the same thing function as if they did' (Mislevy, 1992, p. 72). The important point to emphasise is that the enhanced validity offered by teacher assessments is gained at a cost to consistency and comparability. Moderation is the process of attempting to *enhance* reliability which in technical terms can never be as great as in highly standardised procedures with all pupils taking the same specified tasks.

Enhancing reliability

Where students perform the 'same' task for internal assessment purposes (e.g. a practical maths or science task or an essay with a given title) there are bound to be questions about the comparability of the judgements made by different teachers. Where there is no common task but common assessment criteria or common standards the problem is different but the question the same: can we assume that the assessments are comparable across teachers and institutions?

Quality assurance is an approach that aims for standardisation or consistency of approach, that is it focuses on the process of assessment. Quality control on the other hand focuses on ensuring that the outcomes are judged in a comparable way. Generally these two processes, and others which attempt to support comparability, are termed, in the UK, moderation. I shall now review the most relevant procedure from those outlined in Chapter 1, to explore how it can enhance teacher assessment.

Group moderation

This refers to the moderation of teachers' assessments by the common or consensus judgements of a group or panel of teachers and/or experts or moderators (SSABSA, 1988). This is called variously group, consensus or social moderation, agreement panels or agreement trials. Here I will use the term group moderation. The key point is that it relies on teachers' professional judgement and is essentially concerned with quality assurance and the professional development of teachers, although it may serve a quality control purpose.

In group moderation examples of work are discussed by groups of teachers or lecturers; the purpose is to arrive at shared understandings of the criteria in operation and thus both the processes and the products of assessment are considered. The process can be widened to groups of schools within a district or county: samples of graded work can be brought by one or two teachers from each school to be moderated at the district/county level. This will reveal any discrepancies among the various local groups and the same process of discussion and comparison would lead to some assessments being changed in the same way as at the local level meeting. The teachers then take this information back to their own schools and discuss it in order to achieve a broader consensus.

Meetings across schools (as proposed for the English National Curriculum assessment programme in the TGAT Report, DES 1988) serve to enhance the consistency of judgements at the system level. They are, of course, more costly than meetings within a school/institution, but need to be evaluated in terms of their potential for supporting professional development of teachers particularly in relation to the processes of assessment, what counts as achievement and how it may be best produced. Through discussion the assessments assigned to some pieces of work will be changed: 'The emphasis is on collegial support and the movement towards consensus judgements through social interaction and staff development' (Linn, 1992, p. 25).

> In the use of social (ie 'group') moderation, the comparability of scores assigned depends substantially on the development of a consensus among professionals. The process of verification of a sample of student papers or other products at successively higher levels in the system (e.g. school, district, state, nation) provides a means of broadening the consensus across the boundaries of individual classrooms or schools. It also serves an audit function that is likely to be an essential element in gaining public acceptance.
>
> (Linn, 1992, p. 26)

A prerequisite to this process, of course, is a common marking scheme or a shared understanding of assessment criteria (that is the statements of attainment in National Curriculum assessment). The provision of exemplars, samples of marked or graded work, is sometimes a part of this process and, whilst not doing away with the need to have discussions about levels of performance, does aid teachers in getting an understanding of the overall standards. In National Curriculum assessment at Key Stage 1 in 1991 and 1992 when teachers were given little guidance in how to make their own assessments against the statements of attainment, they found *Children's Work Assessed* booklets (SEAC, 1993) helpful in deciding what counted as evidence of performance for the different statements.

It is important to emphasise that it is not sufficient to focus on consistency of standards in marking or grading. *Consistency of standards* relates to ensuring that different teachers interpret the assessment criteria in the same way. However, it may also be necessary to ensure *consistency of approach*: the assessment task or activity which is used and the way in which such tasks are presented to the pupil, or indeed contextualised, can affect performance quite markedly. To ensure consistency of approach, therefore, we need to ensure that teachers understand fully the constructs which they are assessing (and therefore what sort of tasks to set); how to get at the pupil's knowledge and understanding (and therefore what sort of questions to ask); and how to elicit the pupil's best performance (the physical, social and intellectual context in which the assessment takes place).

Group moderation is a key element of internal assessment, not only in terms of improving inter-marker reliability, but to support the *process* of assessment too. If we wish to be able to 'warrant assessment-based conclusions' without resorting to highly standardised procedures with all that this implies for poor validity, then we must ensure that teachers have common understandings of the criterion performance and the circumstances and contexts which elicit best performance.

The disadvantage of group moderation is that it is time consuming and costly and this may then be seen to add to any unmanageability in an assessment programme. Its great advantage on the other hand lies in its effect on teachers' practice (Linn, 1992; Radnor and Shaw, 1994). It has been found that where teachers come together to discuss performance standards, or criteria, the moderation process becomes a process of teacher development with wash-back on teaching. It seems that coming together to discuss performance or scoring is less personally and professionally threatening than discussing, for example, pedagogy. But discussion of assessment does not end there: issues of production of work follow on and this broadens the scope of discussion and impacts on teaching.

Moderation of teacher assessment in national assessment at Key Stage 1

In the section on moderation in the TGAT Report (DES, 1988) the authors argue for group moderation as the most appropriate method of moderation for National Curriculum assessment because of its emphasis on communication and its ability to value and enhance teachers' professional judgements. However, the detailed account given of how such group moderation must work (paras 73 to 77) makes it clear that the process intended by TGAT is much closer to a scaling process, using the external national test results to adjust the distributions of teachers' assessments.

The procedure proposed was as follows: groups of teachers would meet and consider two sets of results for each element of the National Curriculum: their own ratings and the results on the national tests, both expressed in terms of distributions over the levels of the National Curriculum, e.g. percentages at Levels 1, 2 and 3. The task of the group would be to explore any lack of match between the two distributions. 'The general aim would be to adjust the overall teacher rating results to match the overall results of the national tests' (para. 74). The group would then go on to consider any discrepancies for particular schools using samples of work and knowledge of the circumstances of schools.

> The moderation group's aim would here be to arrive at a final distribution for each school or pupil group. In general this would be the distribution on the national tests, with the implication that teachers' ratings would need adjustment, but departures from this could be approved if the group as a whole could be convinced that they were justified in particular cases.
>
> (DES, 1988, para. 75)

While the Report did accept that the process could be carried out without the need for a group meeting at all (by simply adjusting the distribution to agree with those of the national testing) it argued for the opportunity for teachers to discuss mismatches between internal and external assessments in terms of their interpretation of the National Curriculum itself and the national assessment instruments.

Thus what was being suggested here was a group process which, rather than requiring teachers to bring together pieces of work and agree on a common standard on the basis of their own professional judgements, involved teachers learning to adjust their ratings in the light of the external test results, which are considered to be the absolute standard (except in very occasional situations). Whilst these 'professional deliberations have a valuable staff development function' (para. 76) it hardly looks like an assessment programme which values the professional judgement of teachers. It is essentially a quality control approach which aims to have a quality assurance role in the longer term.

The reaction from the Schools Examination and Assessment Council (SEAC) to the TGAT approach to moderation was negative for four reasons: it would place too many demands on teachers; it would take too long; for some attainment targets there would be no standard assessment task (SAT) data; moderation in a criterion-referenced system should be focused on individuals' scores, rather than scaling the outcomes of groups of pupils (Daugherty, 1994). As Daugherty points out, it was less clear what model of moderation should replace the TGAT one.

In the event at Key Stage 1 a form of moderation by inspection was employed, for teacher assessment and SATs. In National Curriculum assessment Year 2 teachers are required to make an assessment of each pupil's level of attainment on Levels 1–4 of the scale 1–10 in relation to the attainment targets of the core subjects. Teachers may make these assessments in any way they wish, but observation, regular informal assessment and keeping examples of work, are all encouraged. In the first half of the summer term and the second half of the spring term the pupils are given, by their teacher, a series of SATs covering a sample of the core attainment targets. (In future SATs are to be called standard tasks at age seven, and standard tests at eleven and fourteen.)

As James and Conner (1993) point out, the SEAC handbook for moderators emphasised consistency of approach (to conducting the assessments) *and* consistency of standards (inter-rater reliability) which were to be achieved in 1991 and 1992 through the moderation process.

Of major concern in relation to reliability was that the statements of attainment are not always sufficiently clear to allow teachers to make unambiguous judgements about performance; the criteria in this criterion-referenced assessment system were not specific enough for assessment purposes. In some of our research schools, which we describe as analytic, teachers discussed criteria and standards of performance among themselves and in these schools it is likely that assessments were more standardised and more comparable across classes than in other schools (Gipps, 1992b), a finding supported by the official evaluation in 1992 (NFER/BGC, 1992). In the schools where discussion did take place it was partly because of the woolliness of the assessment criteria that these discussions were started. The visiting moderator helped in these discussions in some schools (James and Conner, 1993).

Owing to the problems with the statements of attainment there has been some concern over inter-rater (or judge) reliability. The technical evaluations carried out in 1991 indicate that statements of attainment were indeed interpreted differently by different teachers (NFER/BGC, 1991) and that assessments made of the same attainment target by teacher assessment, SAT and an alternative test had unacceptable levels of variation (Shorrocks *et al.*, 1992). The 1992 evaluation (NFER/BGC,

1992) found that the match between TA levels and SAT levels was significantly greater in the second year of the assessment. A range of factors could be causing this, one at least being an artefact of the system rather than necessarily being due to teachers' changing assessment skills. In 1992 teachers did *not* have to commit themselves to their TA levels until *after* the SATs were completed; it is possible then that the teachers' own assessments were affected by the SAT results; it is also possible that some teachers did not make a separate TA but simply used the SAT result where an attainment target was assessed by both.

The evidence on inter-rater reliability is limited to the comparison of TA and SAT level, which is of dubious value. Furthermore the supervising body, SEAC, has admitted that there were good reasons for TA and SAT results *not* to align. TA, although less standardised, covers a wider range of attainments over a longer period of time, it may be less accurate than SAT assessment but is more thorough and offers a better description of overall attainment. 'The two forms of assessment should not therefore be regarded as identical' (SEAC, 1991, p. 34). The determination of mastery was also an issue in 1991 and 1992: for the SATs all but one statement of attainment had to be achieved to gain a particular level while in TA there was no such rule, and we do not know how teachers made their mastery decisions.

Evidence on inter-rater reliability of the SATs is therefore patchy but there is some evidence (James and Conner, 1993; NFER/BGC, 1992) which our case studies would support that teachers in schools who have, or make, the opportunity to discuss standards of performance, that is engage in group moderation, are developing common standards for assessment. Furthermore, the process of moderation had forced teachers to interact, negotiate meaning for statements of attainment, standardise judgements about individual children and discuss 'levelness' (Brown, Gipps and McCallum, 1993). Concern about wider, national, levels of consistency remain, however.

The process of group moderation, in which groups of teachers with or without a 'moderator', or external expert, come together and discuss pieces of work or what counts as performance, greatly aids comparability. In some schools this process was going on but it needs to be supported and routinised if it is to have any serious impact on teachers' assessments.

From 1993 the process is to be called 'auditing', the term moderation having been dropped (DfE, 1993). The key difference is that rather than offering a system which supports moderation of the process and procedure of the assessments, evidence will be required that results conform to national standards: headteachers will have to ensure that teachers become familiar with national standards and keep evidence of assessment and records for audit when required. It is therefore a process of quality control rather than assurance.

The report by Sir Ron Dearing on the National Curriculum and assessment recognises the role of teacher assessment both for formative purposes and, when moderated, for summative purposes, and recommends giving equal standing to TA and national tests in reporting to parents. The moderation process proposed in the interim report is, however, for a form of statistical moderation with national test results providing the consistency of standards against which to judge TA. National tests will 'iii) provide a means of moderating teacher assessment in the subject so that discrepancies between the outcome of tests and teacher assessment can be investigated *in order to improve teacher assessments*' (Dearing, 1993, emphasis added). In the same vein, Dearing claims that moderation by groups of teachers or through visitation 'cannot readily produce the same consistency of standards as national tests' (Dearing, 1993, p. 50).

We need to move the debate beyond this assertion, since consistency of standards is attainable. Furthermore, we need assessment approaches which balance validity and consistency of standards; teacher assessment properly moderated, as described in this paper, can achieve this and enhance teachers' professional involvement and skills.

Conclusion

Assessment internal to the school in which the teacher is centrally involved is more professionally rewarding (in terms of enhancing teaching and learning) and valid (because of the range of skills and processes which may be included and the range of contexts in which assessment may take place) than external assessment, in which the teacher has little involvement. If, however, such assessment is to be used outside the classroom in reporting to parents or for accountability and certificating purposes, there must be some assurance to those receiving and using the results that there is comparability across teachers, tasks and pupils.

It is possible to ensure this through forms of statistical moderation, inspection of marked work by post and other quality control mechanisms. However, in line with the professional aspect of teacher assessment, forms of moderation which are based on quality assurance and result in teacher development and enhanced understanding of the subject matter and its assessment are to be preferred. Group moderation, which involves discussing criteria as well as pieces of work, what counts as achievement and how such achievement is produced, is the most thorough of the quality assurance approaches. The considerable time (and cost) involved should not be underestimated, but the process can be seen as a valuable aspect of professional development.

Finally, assuring quality through focusing on the processes of assessment and the assessment tasks, will, I believe, lead *ipso facto* to quality control of the outcomes of assessment; this together with an emphasis on validity will lead to confidence in comparability and high-quality assessment.

Note

Aspects of this chapter also appear in Gipps, 1994.

References

Brown, M., Gipps, C. and McCallum, B. (1993) The impact and use of national assessment results. Paper presented to BERA conference, Liverpool, September.

Daugherty, R. (1994) *National Curriculum Assessment: A Review of Policy 1988–1993*, Falmer, Lewes.

Dearing, Sir R. (1993) *The National Curriculum and its Assessment: Interim Report*, July, NCC and SEAC, London.

DES (Department of Education and Science) (1988) *National Curriculum Task Group on Assessment and Testing – A Report*, DES/WO, London.

DfE (Department for Education) (1993) *The Education (Assessment Arrangements for the Core Subjects) (Key Stage 1) Order 1993*, Circular 11/93, DfE, London.

Gipps, C. (1992a) *What We Know About Effective Primary Teaching*, London File/Tufnell Press, London. Reprinted in Bourne, J. (ed.) (1994) *Thinking Through Primary Practice* Open University/ Routledge, London.

Gipps, C. (1992b) National testing at seven: what can it tell us? Paper presented at AERA Conference, San Francisco.

Gipps, C. (1994) *Beyond Testing? Towards a Theory of Educational Assessment*, Falmer, Lewes.

James, M. and Conner, C. (1993) Are reliability and validity achievable in National Curriculum assessment? Some observations on moderation at Key Stage One in 1992, *The Curriculum Journal*, Vol. 4, no. 1, pp. 5–19.

Linn, R. L. (1992) Linking results of distinct assessments. Unpublished, CRESST, UCLA, August.

McCallum, E., McAlister, S., Brown, M. and Gipps, C. (1993) Teacher assessment at Key Stage One, *Research Papers in Education*, Vol. 8, no. 3, pp. 305–27.

Mislevy, R. J. (1992) *Linking Educational Assessments. Concepts, Issues, Methods and Prospects*, Educational Testing Services, Princeton.

NFER/BGC (National Foundation for Educational Research/Bishop Grossetest College) (1991) *An Evaluation of National Curriculum Assessment*, Report 3, June.

NFER/BGC (National Foundation for Educational Research/Bishop Grosetest College) (1992) *An Evaluation of the 1992 National Curriculum Assessment at IKSI*, September.

Radnor, H. and Shaw, K. (1994 in press) Developing a collaborative approach to moderation: the moderation and assessment project – south west, in Torrance, H. (ed.) *Evaluating Authentic Assessment*, Open University Press, Buckingham.

Sadler, R. (1989) Formative assessment and the design of instructional systems, *Instructional Science*, Vol. 18, pp. 119–44.

SEAC (School Examination and Assessment Council) (1991) *National Curriculum Assessment at Key Stage 3: A Review of the 1991 Pilots with Implications for 1992*, EMU: SEAC, London.

SEAC (School Examination and Assessment Council) (1993) *School Assessment Folder*, Children's Work Assessed, SEAC, London.

SSABSA (Senior Secondary Assessment Board of South Australia) (1988) *Assessment and Moderation Policy*, Information Booklet no. 2, SSABSA, South Australia.

Shorrocks, D., Daniels, S., Frobisher, L., Nelson, N., Waterson, A. and Bell, J. (1992) *ENCA 1 Project Report*, SEAC, London.

5

THE QUALITY OF ASSESSMENT IN FURTHER EDUCATION IN SCOTLAND

Harry Black

An advantage of being small is that matters can be less complicated. Scottish education has that advantage. Although until the early 1980s Scottish further education (FE) suffered from the plethora of awarding bodies which is still to be found in England and Wales, since then the Scottish Vocational Education Council (SCOTVEC) has been the sole body responsible for the accreditation and award of Scottish vocational qualifications. Furthermore, partly because of scale and also because of the strong influence of the Scottish Office in nurturing a clear indepen-dent identity for Scottish education, there has been much commonality in aspirations and in the form of delivery across Scottish colleges. As a consequence, provided it is seen as acceptable by teaching staff and those with responsibility for college management, change can be rapid.

One of the best examples of the way in which this commonality of purpose led to change is to be found in the rapid development of new assessment and certification systems in the 1980s. In the 1970s the need for change in assessment and certification in schools was widely recog-nised (SED, 1977) and this led to a substantial shift towards criterion-referenced assessment. It was quickly recognised that the same rationale could and should be applied in further education (SED, 1983).

In a number of ways the changes brought about in further education were even more radical than those which were taking place in secondary schools. Out went a tradition of full courses assessed largely by external examinations on an essentially norm-referenced basis and in came a diet

Copyright © 1994, Harry Black

of forty-hour modules described by module descriptors which set out the criteria to be assessed and the assessment procedures to be used and left the responsibility for criterion-referenced decisions on competence firmly in the hands of the colleges and their staff. By the time SCOTVEC was formally established in 1985, 1,700 different 'National Certificate' module descriptors had been written and by the end of the decade there were around 2,500 available. Since then the Council has replaced the structure of its former Higher National Certificate (HNC) and Diploma (HND) awards with a set of modular Higher National Units and also developed a series of Workplace Assessed Units. It has packaged various permutations of National Certificate modules, Higher National Units and Workplace Assessed Units as National Certificate clusters, General Scottish Vocational Qualifications, National Certificate Group Awards and Scottish Vocational Qualifications. At the same time individual students can still opt to study one National Certificate module or a small group of them which meet their particular interests and these are recorded on their own record of education and training provided by SCOTVEC.

It is another feature of Scottish education that it is relatively open to scrutiny. As part of its own observation of the effects of these rapid changes on various aspects of further education, the Scottish Office Education Department commissioned a series of independent research studies from the Scottish Council for Research in Education (Black, Hall and Yates, 1988; Black *et al.*, 1989; Black, Hall and Martin, 1991, 1992). The focus and function of these varied, but a recurring theme concerned the quality of the assessments which were being made and the views which teaching staff and others had of this.

The main purpose of this chapter is to record some of the insights which developed from that series of projects – which for convenience will be referred to by their date of publication. Some of the issues which emerged in that 'formative' stage of the particular programmes evaluated may no longer apply not least because a purpose of the research was to illuminate these and subsequent policy changes will hopefully have addressed them. However, at a more general level, the evidence would suggest that a number of themes emerged which might well apply to other attempts to implement criterion-referenced certification systems. The main value of the studies may therefore be that they provide a detailed 'case study' of the challenge which such a shift represents.

A pattern of change

There was an interesting similarity between staff views in the 1988 and 1992 studies on the early years of the National Certificate and Higher

National Unit developments respectively. In both, while college staff were hesitant about several details of the model they were being asked to adopt, they welcomed the changes in principle and rejected the option of reverting to the systems they had replaced. Given our additional experience of working with schoolteachers introducing and implementing Standard Grade examinations (Black and Devine, 1986; Black *et al.*, 1988; Hall, Fenwick and Black, 1994; Devine, Black and Gray, 1994), our hypothesis was that there may be a pattern of staff perceptions on the acceptability of moving from 'norm-referenced', 'general attainment' models of assessment towards 'criterion-references', 'competence-based' approaches. Overall, we felt that three stages of response could be identified: initial enthusiasm for the basic principles prior to implementation because of the perceived educational benefits; mixed reactions when staff face up to the realities of implementation; and finally systematic adaptation as the 'new' system becomes the status quo and staff begin to develop the experience, understanding and confidence to deal with their problems. Here we take this hypothesis a stage further and identify some of the perceptions and concerns which seem to typify each stage. In the third stage the focus will be on some of the issues which seem to have persisted as problematic and which may therefore be the most intractable for institutionally assessed criterion-referenced certification systems in general.

Stage one – initial reactions

Brown (1988) identified a number of themes which typify contemporary innovation in assessment practice. These comprise:

- a broadening of the concept of assessment away from 'testing' for certification purposes towards strategies which are more closely integrated with the curriculum and which fulfil multiple purposes;
- an increase in the range of qualities assessed and the contexts in which assessment takes place;
- a shift towards criterion-referenced descriptive assessment and away from relying on marks or grades which have little value other than in comparison with others;
- a devolution of the responsibility for assessment to schools and colleges;
- a commitment to making certification available to a much greater proportion of the population than has been the case in the past.

Experience suggests that assessment innovations which share these characteristics have been well received by teachers. Both the National Certificate and Higher National Unit developments which are the subject of this paper have these characteristics. It is sometimes difficult to distinguish between the assessment specifications and the statement of curriculum in the module descriptors; staff are encouraged to use assessments for both formative and summative purposes; the range of competences on which assessment focuses has increased substantially and is now essentially skill based rather than knowledge based; the model of assessment is clearly criterion referenced and college based; the policy of allowing access to certification through a range of routes offers the opportunity for involvement to many who were hitherto excluded.

It is hardly surprising therefore that once teaching staff had come to terms with the need to change, the direction in which these changes took them was broadly welcomed. However, even at this early stage a number of difficulties emerged in both the 1988 and 1992 studies which were universal.

Overall, however, in both of these innovations, and indeed in the parallel 'Standard Grade' implementation which was taking place in schools, the early response was typified more by coming to terms with the meaning of the changes rather than overt antagonism to them. Whether this was because of the way in which they were implemented, because of the unique characteristics of the Scottish educational system, or because of the inherit professional merit of the models adopted is difficult to ascertain. It is, however, a matter of historical fact that despite these changes taking place at a time of considerable industrial unrest, their introduction was not traumatic and their implementation progressed with relatively few modifications.

Stage two – professional challenges

We characterised views in the second stage of implementation as being dominated by mixed reactions when staff face up to the realities of implementation. Essentially this was the stage when the difficulties of implementing a criterion-referenced system emerged and professional solutions were found to circumvent the difficulties.

Two major issues dominated the views staff shared with us at that stage. These comprised particular difficulties which staff had in interpreting the performance criteria which define competence and more general concerns about the nature of module descriptors which are fundamental in sharing understanding about the domains to be assessed.

Performance criteria

Teachers varied in the way in which they were interpreting performance criteria. In some cases, for example typewriting, teachers felt that with the exemplar materials available there is little scope for doubt about the level of performance required to achieve the learning outcome. In other situations, however, there was more cause for concern. In the 1988 study, a personal and social development module was encountered which was being delivered to 'mature adult students'. Because of the lecturer's assumptions about this group, a higher level of performance was required than would have been expected from what he called 'normal' FE students. In another study, the delivery of several building and decorating modules to Youth Training Scheme (YTS) students was seen as causing problems for staff. At one level they wanted to maintain standards which they saw as acceptable to the building trade while at the same time they wished to give recognition to students whom they saw as 'less able'. In a 'trowel skills' module one lecturer interpreted the appropriate part of the performance criteria ('to an acceptable standard and in an agreed time where appropriate') in such a way as to encompass the wide attainment range of the group. In building a short length of wall a tolerance of plus or minus 6 mm was expected of those regarded as the 'better' students, plus or minus 8 mm for the 'average' students and plus or minus 10 mm for the 'less able'. We called this rationalisation of performance criteria according to the characteristics of the group 'individual-referenced' or 'group-referenced' approaches and questioned their appropriateness.

Another set of difficulties arose from the imprecise language used in some descriptors. In a personal and social development (PSD) module on contemporary issues, the groupwork criteria included such phrases as 'respond constructively to others', make 'relevant contributions' and make 'use of appropriate evidence'. All of these require value judgements by the lecturer. There was no guidance on how to interpret them and discussions with staff suggested that they were less than clear. Similar problems were recognised in the 1992 study by the staff themselves:

> You get three or four people round a table and they have three or four ideas about what the performance criteria standard would be like. That's where we've had the problem with the specifications. We think we know what we're about but when we sit down and start talking about it we've clearly got different ideas of how difficult we should make it and I should say that's the biggest difficulty.

Some staff in the 1991 study were also concerned that the assessment requirements of modules were too simple. One maths lecturer observed that the advice and guidance he had received on techniques of assessment had concentrated on the 'lower end of the scale' and there was little or nothing available about assessing higher levels of ability.

Yet another difficulty identified by staff in the 1989 study was uncertainty as to whether 'master' meant 'can do' or 'has done'. Our data suggested that this could be a source of unreliability. An associated problem which was identified in the 1988 study was staff unease about whether mastery was the same if it was displayed in the first instance or only after the teacher had provided additional help. Clearly such problems of definition suggested the need for greater clarification.

A feature of what we considered to be the second stage of implementation was that staff came to develop professional strategies to circumvent their difficulties. We encountered a number of these which are of some interest.

One type of approach was to share the criteria as much as possible with the students themselves. In a communications department in the 1988 study, the performance criteria were displayed on the walls for all to see and to discuss amongst themselves: 'It's not just that we're familiarising the students with them, we are familiarising ourselves with them as we go along.' In both the 1988 and 1989 studies we also encountered examples of what we came to call 'industrial-referencing'. In a caring skills course, lecturers made comparisons with other groups of students with whom placement supervisors would be familiar in order to explain the performance criteria to them: 'Their benchmark was the skills that a student or pupil nurse should have. It's a standard of basic competence – not the same standard as a social worker dealing with clients or a nurse dealing with clients. It's a very elementary level.' Other lecturers clarified the standards they were looking for by referring outside the National Certificate to the requirements in industry or to the commercial criteria they had used when working in industry: 'From an industrial point of view the assessments must be compatible with commercial qualifications.' We found it difficult to take issue with these coping strategies, and indeed if they do in fact lead to better understanding because they fit assessors' experiences then they may be worth building on.

Overall it was clear that from an early stage SCOTVEC and other agencies responsible for supporting these developments recognised the need to help staff to interpret assessment advice. One approach from the 'centre' was to supply examples of graded answers from what was then the Curriculum Advice and Support Team (CAST). Our 1989 study also highlighted the potential role of local support. This study considered the comparability of assessment decisions within and between colleges. In this we encountered a number of disturbingly low levels of agreement in mathematics and stock control modules when assessment instruments were exchanged between departments and colleges. However, when a comparison was made between lecturers' assessments of communication competences across a number of colleges, a high level of agreement was revealed. Analysis suggested that the level of support available was partly responsible for these differences.

In the mathematics and stock control studies there was little evidence of staff sharing their experiences or exchanging their instruments. However, in the colleges in which the communication modules were evaluated, the local authority which was then responsible for them had established a working group which met monthly to review progress. The evidence suggested that this forum had helped staff to develop a common understanding of the performance criteria which had a clear and beneficial influence on the quality of assessment.

Module descriptors

Since the earliest days of criterion-referenced assessment, the central importance and the considerable difficulty of providing robust but economical statements of what is to be assessed has been recognised (Popham and Lindheim, 1980; Berk, 1980). The SCOTVEC approach was to provide National Certificate module descriptors which initially covered the type and purpose of the module, preferred entry level, learning outcomes, content and context, suggested learning and teaching approaches and assessment procedures; and Higher National Unit specifications which initially covered the general competence for the unit, an access statement, credit value, outcomes and associated performance criteria, context and criteria for pass and merit awards. As would have been expected, these proved to be of major importance as staff came to implement the new approaches.

The early 'knee-jerk' reaction of staff, either because they were unfamiliar with the approach or because early versions of descriptors were unpolished or perhaps in some cases because they were genuinely poor, was obvious in some staff comments on descriptors associated with the early implementation of both the National Certificate modules and Higher National Units:

> Some of the [National Certificate] descriptors are written in unclear terms – clarity is certainly lacking – the communication descriptors are an example of how not to communicate and they're a nightmare to administer.

> A senior lecturer with responsibility for support of new part-time and untrained staff I have to 'translate' into normal English all too often the assessment and performance criteria parts of [National Certificate] module descriptors.

> It would appear as if they have just sort of pulled as much as they can from a wide range of references and stuck it into this [Higher National Unit] and to me it's like trying to put a quart into a pint pot. I think that's just overloaded.

Obscure technical language was also seen to be a problem. In some cases this was held to be quite different from the language used by subject specialists. Particular problems arose from the unfamiliarity of expressing things in competence terms and the difficulty of adhering to guidelines on writing outcomes issued by SCOTVEC:

> Writing units is a linguistic exercise. You don't simply write down what they have to do, you have to translate it into competence terms which means what language you are allowed to use. The whole language that all of us are used to – 'know' and 'understand' and being able to 'remember' – suddenly you weren't allowed to have that. And even phrases such as 'explain' and 'justify', some of that was a bit sort of stretching the language.

More helpful insights came from staff who tried to identify what they saw to be the 'ideal' qualities of specifications. In addition to dealing with the problems of clarity and accessibility noted above, it was thought that a specification should not attempt to cover too much content, it should not demand too much assessment and it should have a 'structure' (by which some respondents appeared to mean that one outcome should follow on naturally from another).

In the 1992 study, clear majorities of respondents felt it appropriate for the outcomes to be defined in advance and for the levels of attainment for pass and merit awards to be given. Most preferred that teaching methods and content of teaching be left to the colleges and there was a reasonably even division of opinion about whether assessment instruments and the context of the teaching should be specified. Further education college staff were more inclined to want both the competences and the assessment instruments to be defined in advance while higher education staff showed a greater tendency to want these to be left to their discretion. Presumably this reflects the greater historical reliance on nationally developed courses in FE colleges and the greater familiarity of those staff with the National Certificate modules.

In considering how awarding bodies might deal with the complex challenge of descriptor design, we found it useful to distinguish between assessment problems which could be avoided by using a different approach, and those which are an inevitable consequence of the fundamental design. The clarity possible within module descriptors is in fact a function of both of these.

Whilst in many cases it would have been possible to improve these specifications by writing them more clearly or by giving better examples, there are limits to how much could be achieved in this way. At a pragmatic level, experience suggests that it will be counterproductive to burden teachers with overelaborate descriptors. At a more fundamental level, it may be that the particular model promoted by SCOTVEC contains an element of *inevitable* lack of precision. This arises from the tension between the flexibility, which was intended to be built into both National Certificate modules and Higher National Units, and the aspiration to write tight domain definitions. Modules and units were intended to be 'flexible' enough to cover a range of vocational areas and purposes. It follows that the content specifications have to be defined in fairly general terms in order to leave room for different interpretations which separate vocational areas might require. This 'room for manoeuvre' may inevitably lead to a certain amount of slackness and definition. Overall the question must be how much are we prepared to pay for high reliability.

Stage three – systematic adaptation

In the final stage of staff response, which we described as 'systematic adaptation', the 'new' system had become the status quo and staff had begun to develop the experience, understanding and confidence to deal with their problems. Our final study of National Certificate module delivery suggested that most staff were already in that category (Black *et al.*, 1991).

What characterised this? The most obvious feature was that assessment matters had diminished in priority and staff were generally confident of their skills. Despite this a number of concerns which we had picked up in the early stages of the developments had persisted. Bureaucratic demands were still seen to be excessive and some still felt that too much time was being spent on assessment and too little on teaching. These problems hardly seem inevitable and it was surprising that some did not feel that they had been addressed. There was also a continuing concern amongst staff teaching National Certificate programmes about the extent to which 'standards' were being maintained. By standards they meant comparability amongst assessments of the same learning outcomes made by different staff in different colleges or by the same staff at different times, that is, the reliability of the assessments: 'I do not believe that assessment guidelines are sufficiently specific to ensure a national standard. Why does SCOTVEC not provide a bank of questions from which we can draw assessment material?'

It is important to recognise that these views were collected at a stage when SCOTVEC was in the process of implementing its current quality assurance strategies. In 1989 SCOTVEC issued a consultative document on quality assurance in which they set out their plans for increasing devolution of responsibility to colleges subject to audit. This was followed in 1991 by a policy paper on their quality development programme which presented a framework for the development of quality assurance systems. In this framework they defined the elements of quality assurance as the validation of awards, approval of centres and the verification of assessment (SCOTVEC, 1989, 1991).

There is little in the research data available relating to the validation of awards and the approval of centres. Suffice it to say that staff expressed few reservations about these aspects of the system. The 1992 study showed that staff had both positive and negative views on their experience of course validation. The positive view stemmed from what was seen as the sound professional experience which justifying and defending one's course tended to be. The negative perception was that in some instances, members of validation committees were unclear about the limits of their authority or were overzealous in their criticisms. These comments were gathered in the early days of the introduction of the Higher National Units and certainly not when staff could be said to be in 'stage three' of adaptation.

In the 1992 study, staff had few comments about internal quality assurance and generally appeared reasonably happy with it. The description of the system in one college was that

> Internally we have two bodies which are responsible for overviewing the course. The job of the first really is to look at assessments, to handle problems associated with student appeals. They are also the first filter on proposed assessments, in other words what, in old-fashioned terms, we called a moderating committee. The second level is the course committee. That's a more generalised approach. Above that it gradually gets more diffuse as we report upwards, ultimately to the academic board.

Apart from the internal quality assurance mechanisms which colleges were encouraged to adopt and the staff training modules on assessment which staff were able to undertake, the main responsibility for the verification of assessment was in the hands of external course assessors. In the early stages at least, despite these appointments, the same issue emerged:

> External moderation is a disaster. It doesn't happen. How do I know as a parent that the piece of paper that I get with my youngster having taken a particular module at college A has got the same currency as my friend's youngster who is at college Y doing the same module. That's the worry. That's the big issue at the moment. How are we going to ensure national standards.

My worry is that we are all doing this on our own. I don't know if the standard throughout the country is going to be even at all.

Is there a national policy? I don't know. I could be using standards in this college which are far higher than others or indeed far lower.

Despite these worries it was apparent that individual external course assessors tended to be well regarded both as academic peers and useful sources of advice and guidance:

I think there is a national standard. I think if there was a drastic difference in standards I am sure these people [external course assessors] would pick it up very quickly.

There's a more personal relationship with the external assessor. It's personal in the sense that the assessor is visiting the college, represented on the committee, and we found ours very amenable to giving advice, guidance and support. We have found our external assessors very helpful if we want to sound out ideas.

Overall the balance of opinion on the efficacy of external course assessors in maintaining cross-college comparability was even. However, the opinion was also expressed that external course assessors were extremely important but were being asked to perform an almost impossible task.

I think external examiners or external assessors are very important from the viewpoint of maintaining parity of level of achievement of students in any institutions anywhere. The working relationships we have with our external course assessors have been excellent. If you tell an assessor that he has two days a year in any one institution and you ask him to moderate all the assessment used as part of the course as described in competence terms, you've actually described a wholly ludicrous position. I think that the system as it stands, as I understood from the SCOTVEC prospective, is unworkable for assessors. They can't do the job that SCOTVEC wants them to do.

Conclusion

This chapter has described more than five years of experience in tracking the implementation of what is arguably one of the best-known examples of applying a criterion-referenced assessment model to a high-stakes national assessment system. That system has also broken new ground in British education by devolving the responsibility for assessment almost entirely to individual institutions and teachers.

The data available from these studies strongly suggest that even in the relatively short period of time that the systems have been in place, they have been broadly welcomed by staff and largely assimilated into their professional practice. There have been many difficulties along the way, particularly in describing the content of the modules through their specification and establishing criteria for assessment through performance criteria. The evidence would seem to be that some of these problems are avoidable and that others can be ameliorated particularly by strategies which encourage staff to share their understandings and their difficulties.

Of greater concern, however, was some evidence of certain difficulties, and particularly that of persuading teaching staff that a 'national standard' of comparability between the assessments of staff in different colleges has been established. This appears to be the case despite the considerable effort which SCOTVEC, which is responsible for the system, has put into establishing quality assurance mechanisms.

From an assessment perspective, clearly such matters are resoluble. Inter-rater reliability is easy to establish at a theoretical level particularly where there is an element of written work available. Even in contexts where assessments rely on the observation of behaviour, the techniques of moderation are perfectly straightforward if a little cumbersome. But it is equally clear that in a system in which millions of individual assessment decisions are made by teaching staff throughout the country and at different times throughout the year, the cost implications of using such approaches are prohibitive.

There are of course alternatives. Perhaps the most obvious would be to involve an element of external assessment and the most recent evidence from research on Standard Grade assessments (Devine *et al.*, 1994; Hall *et al.*, 1994) suggests that this would reflect a high level of agreement with teacher assessments. Many would consider that to be a step backwards and it would at any rate be difficult to achieve in a system which requires module assessments to be conducted throughout the year. SCOTVEC has instead opted for a quality assurance system which relies heavily on building the professional competence of college staff and establishing verification 'lightly' through external course assessors. This pragmatic solution fits better in resource terms than alternative 'heavy' external verification of individual assessment decisions. Whether it will be sufficient to persuade teaching staff that their concerns about 'national standards' are unfounded will only be known in time. Whether it is sufficient to achieve the comparability which would warrant such a claim could only be verified by further research.

References

Berk, R. A. (1980) (ed.) *Criterion-Referenced Measurement*, Johns Hopkins University Press, Baltimore.

Black, H. D. and Devine, M. (1986) *Assessment Purposes*, The Scottish Council for Research in Education, Edinburgh.

Black, H. D., Devine, M., Turner, E. and Harrison, C. (1988) *Standard Grade Assessment: A Support Package for Schools*, The Scottish Council for Research in Education, Edinburgh.

Black, H. D., Hall, J. and Martin, S. (1991) *Modules: Teaching, Learning and Assessment. The Views of Students, Staff and Employers Involved in the National Certificate*, The Scottish Council for Research in Education, Edinburgh.

Black, H. D., Hall, J. and Martin, S. (1992) *Units and Competence: A Case Study of SCOTVEC's Advanced Courses Development Programme*, The Scottish Council for Research in Education, Edinburgh.

Black, H. D., Hall, J. Martin, S. and Yates, J. (1989) *The Quality of Assessment: Case Studies in the National Certificate*, The Scottish Council for Research in Education, Edinburgh.

Black, H. D., Hall, J. and Yates, J. (1988) *Assessing Modules; Staff Perceptions of Assessment for the National Certificate*, The Scottish Council for Research in Education, Edinburgh.

Brown, S. (1988) (ed.) *Assessment: A Changing Practice*, Scottish Academic Press, Edinburgh.

Devine, M., Black, H. and Gray, D. (1994) *Standard Grade Mathematics: Achievements and Competences*, The Scottish Council for Research in Education, Edinburgh.

Hall, J., Fenwick, N. and Black, H. D. (1994) *Standard Grade English: Achievements and Competences*, The Scottish Council for Research in Education, Edinburgh.

Popham, W. J. and Lindheim, E. (1980) *The Practical Side of CRT Development*, NCME Measurement in Education Series, Vol. 10, no. 4, Spring 1980.

SED (Scottish Education Department) (1977) *Assessment for All – Report of the Committee to Review Assessment in the Third and Fourth Years of Secondary Education in Scotland*, HMSO, Edinburgh.

SED (Scottish Education Department) (1983) *16–18's in Scotland: An Action Plan*, HMSO, Edinburgh.

SCOTVEC (Scottish Vocational Education Council) (1989) *Quality Assurance: A Consultative Paper*, Scottish Vocational Education Council, Glasgow.

SCOTVEC (Scottish Vocational Education Council) (1991) *Quality Development Programme Policy Paper*, Scottish Vocational Education Council, Glasgow.

6

QUALITY ASSURANCE, TEACHER ASSESSMENTS AND PUBLIC EXAMINATIONS

Richard Daugherty

Public examinations for secondary school students in the UK have seen a trend until recently towards increasing reliance on assessments undertaken by the students' teachers during the course of study. Such 'coursework assessment', from being an innovative feature of the Certificate of Secondary Education (CSE) introduced in England and Wales in 1965, has been extended so that it has become a significant element in the assessment of many courses, especially those leading to the certification of sixteen-year-olds (Kingdon and Stobart, 1988).

The focus of this chapter is on the General Certificate of Secondary Education (GCSE), introduced in England, Wales and Northern Ireland in 1986 as a replacement for the General Certificate of Education (GCE) O-level and the CSE. Its counterpart in Scotland, the Standard Grade examination, which replaced the Ordinary Grade over a phasing-in period from 1984 through to 1992, has also seen the increased use of assessment by teachers. For Standard Grade, one of the three 'elements' defined in each subject is internally assessed and externally moderated with about one-third of schools having their assessments checked each year.

The use of coursework assessment in all types of public examination has been advocated because of the gains in validity which can be expected when students' performance on assessed tasks can be judged in a greater range of contexts and more frequently than is possible within the constraints of time-limited, written examinations. The list of 'aspects of

Copyright © 1994, Richard Daugherty

attainment which may not easily or adequately be tested by [examination] papers' listed in *Coursework Assessment in GCSE* (SEC, 1985) is one example of the ways in which the case for coursework assessment has been presented during the past three decades. Extracts from this list are quoted in Chapter 1 (p. 14).

But the use of evidence obtained during the course by teachers as a component in the final grading would be called into question if the reliability of those assessments were not demonstrably sufficiently robust for the user of the certificate to have confidence in it. As has been argued earlier (Chapter 1, p. 15), 'the matter of reliability must be faced, for . . . an unreliable assessment is not only of little use but can be unjust'. The focus here is on reliability – 'the results of the assessment should be consistent over assessors and occasions' – and on comparability – 'the results of the assessment should be consistent from centre to centre, and on a national basis' (Nuttall and Thomas, 1993, p. 3). These considerations are discussed as they apply to a particular cohort of students being assessed rather than to the 'cross-moderation' procedures which may be implemented to monitor and adjust over time the consistency of the judgements made by separate but parallel groups of examiners (Goldstein, 1986).

The procedures established to maximise reliability in circumstances where assessment decisions are made by teachers, are central to the quality of assessment in wholly or partially school-based examinations. This was acknowledged as a central issue from the earliest days of the development of the CSE. The stated purpose of the Schools Council examination bulletin no. 5, published in 1965, was 'to suggest a possible approach to the problems of moderation which are likely to arise with internal, or school-based, examinations' (Schools Council, 1965, p. 1). More recently, as criticism of the extent of reliance on coursework assessment has grown, in particular in England, the nature and adequacy of moderation procedures are being more closely scrutinised, both professionally and in the context of a wider debate about the place of coursework in public examinations.

Coursework and the GCSE

The examinations which GCSE replaced made varying, though steadily increasing, use of coursework but it was to become one of the defining features of the new examination. As expressed in *Better Schools* (DES/WO, 1985a) the changes in assessment practice were very clear: 'by comparison with existing examinations, the [GCSE] national criteria place a new emphasis on oral and practical skills and coursework'

(p. 30). Syllabuses across all subjects, with few exceptions, were required to make provision for a minimum 20 per cent of the credit available to students to come from work done during the course and assessed by the students' own teachers – 'school-based assessment'. For the first batch of syllabuses, in use from 1986, no upper limit was placed on the proportion of credit obtainable from such assessment. In some subjects, notably English, syllabuses with 100 per cent coursework assessment were devised, approved and widely adopted by schools.

An examination which depended, even only in part, on the judgement of teachers was from the outset the subject of criticism by those who argue for externally set and marked examinations as the only reliable means of measuring attainment (North, 1987). Criticism from the Right of the Conservative Party, comparing the GCSE unfavourably with GCE O-level, has often been strident: 'Eventually, interested parties would come to realise which examination system was the most reliable as a test of a student's achievements and abilities, and which systems were (as the GCSE promises to be) little more than an award offered by a teacher to himself' (Hillgate Group, 1987, p. 20). Some professional concerns about coursework assessment were also voiced in the early years of GCSE, especially when prompted by reports from HM Inspectorate. Initially, the HMI verdict on coursework was broadly favourable: 'The gains which have accrued in quality of work and improved assessment from integrated assessed coursework outweigh the many problems which have arisen' (HMI, 1988, p. 6). There was, however, sufficient pressure on ministers for limits to be introduced to the extent of reliance on coursework, with a maximum of 70 per cent being stipulated in 1990, to come into effect from 1992.

But the cutting back of coursework so that 100 per cent coursework schemes would no longer be permitted was insufficient to stifle criticism from those who, for ideological or more pragmatic reasons, remained unconvinced about an award which still depended substantially on in-course judgements by teachers. Another bout of public criticism in 1992, again prompted by an HMI report and fuelled by a sympathetic Secretary of State for Education, led to further limitations, variable across subjects, on coursework assessment. What had been a *minimum* percentage for GCSE coursework in 1986 – 20 per cent – was to become a *maximum* in several of the main subjects from 1994 as this latest revision of government policy on the use of teacher assessments took effect.

The technical challenges of ensuring the reliability of coursework assessment remained as a continuing responsibility of the examining boards. But, by 1992, the technical issues were being discussed against the background of an increasingly politicised debate about the merits of teacher assessments (in the context of the National Curriculum at other 'Key Stages' as well as in relation to the GCSE).

Moderation and the GCSE

While the term 'moderation' can be applied to the process of approving and/or marking examination papers, it is used here to refer to the ways in which the assessment decisions of teachers, arrived at in the context of the school-based assessment component of a public examination, can be brought into a relationship with each other so that they can contribute to the grades awarded in that examination.

In her study *School-Based Assessment in GCE and CSE Boards*, Harris (1986) noted:

> there is some variation in what is understood by the term itself. Comparability is the key element: the need to equate the marks of different teachers in different schools with one another . . .
> . . . moderation is defined as a means of ensuring comparability between teachers' marks and, just as curriculum should be considered concomitantly with assessment, so should assessment be considered alongside methods of moderation.
>
> (Harris, 1986, p. 129)

Moderation of school-based assessments became a central issue with the decision that there should be a minimum of 20 per cent school-based assessment in GCSE syllabuses. The glossary of terms issued as an appendix to the GCSE general criteria (DES/WO, 1985b) defined moderation as (p. 23) 'the process of aligning standards between different examinations, different components or (most frequently) different centres or teachers responsible for the assessment of their own candidates'.

If only indirectly, the general criteria thus referred to the question of at which point or points within the process of school-based assessment the procedures designed to align standards might be required. Within any one scheme of examining in one subject administered by one examination board, the consistency of standard across teachers in the same school and across teachers in all schools entering candidates could be the focus of attention. In a scheme with a large candidate entry, comparability of standard across several moderators, each responsible for a proportion of centres, might be an issue. Broader questions of comparability come into play when considering the practice in the same subject of different examining bodies or practice across different subjects. Awareness of the potential for variability arising at several points within the examining process leads to recognition that, to be fully effective, moderation of school-based assessment must necessarily impact upon that process at several points between the publication of a syllabus (for the teacher, the official 'ground rules') and the eventual award of grades to candidates.

By the time the original general criteria had been superseded by new regulations including a *Glossary of Terms* (SEAC, 1992a) the extended 200-plus word clarification of the term of which the above extract forms a part had been reduced to eight words (p. 5): 'the process of aligning standards of internal assessment'.

Moderation methods

By the 1970s the methods used in public examinations to align standards of internal assessment had been extensively and variously developed across examination boards and across many of the subjects examined. A survey and review published in 1977 is testimony to the progress made over the previous decade (Cohen and Deale, 1977).

A similar range of methods is reported in Harris's survey of school-based assessment (Harris, 1986) in the pre-GCSE circumstances of GCE O-level and CSE. Her report remains the most recent published account of practice in this respect in the public examinations of England and Wales. Writing in the context of developing moderating instruments for vocational examinations, Nuttall and Thomas (1993) have also reviewed trends in moderation methods in public examinations, in particular the decline of statistically based procedures.

The Secondary Examinations Council booklet based on the Harris report (SEC, 1986) draws attention to the special features of moderating teachers' assessments (p. 6): 'Such a procedure [moderation] is a famil-iar feature of external examining although two factors are peculiar to school-based assessment – firstly, the scale of the exercise; and secondly, that teachers are automatically assessors.' Two main forms of modera-tion are defined – statistical moderation and moderation by inspection – though the latter category is subdivided (p. 7): 'Moderation by inspec-tion . . . can mean sending a sample of all of candidates' work to a moderator; or it can mean a consortium or local group meeting; or it can mean a moderator visiting a centre – the latter most common when the product or process is bulky or ephemeral.' 'Ephemeral' draws attention to a third central feature of school-based assessment, the likelihood that there will be some attainments defined in terms of a process and having no 'product' on which the judgement of a second assessor – colleague, peer group member, external moderator – can focus.

The original general criteria for the GCSE (DES/WO, 1985b) make the same distinction between 'statistical moderation' and 'moderation by inspection', going into considerable detail about the criteria for systems of assessment and moderation. Even its glossary touches on appropriateness of methodology:

> The most appropriate form of moderation to be used in a particular examination will depend on the circumstances of the nature of the examination or component being moderated. If statistical moderation against an externally assessed component is to be used it is essential that there is a satisfactory level of correlation between the internally assessed component being moderated and the externally assessed components used to moderate it.
>
> (DES/WO, 1985b, p. 23)

The well-established difficulty of using reference tests to moderate school-based assessment (Nuttall and Thomas, 1993, p. 7) is thus hinted at rather than clarified.

In establishing the framework for National Curriculum assessment the Task Group on Assessment and Testing (TGAT) (DES/WO, 1988) approached the question of moderation from a different direction. The TGAT discussion of alternative methods emphasised moderation's function in informing how teachers would arrive at their judgements as much as the more familiar function of aligning the judgements of teachers after the event:

> Methods of moderation have twin functions: to communicate general standards to individual assessors and to control aberrations from general standards by appropriate adjustments. Three methods are in common use:
> — scaling on a reference test;
> — inspection by visiting moderators;
> — group moderation bringing teachers together to discuss their assessments.
> Each differs in its relative emphasis on communication and control.
>
> (DES/WO, 1988, para. 68)

How quality assurance is interpreted in National Curriculum assessment is discussed elsewhere (Chapters 4 and 7). It is interesting, however, to note in passing that the issue of how to align standards in national assessment at Key Stages 1 and 3 seems to have been debated alongside, but largely separately from, the debate about the equivalent and longer established procedures in use in public examinations for older students.

Moderation practice in the GCSE

Over the period when the arrangements for assessing pupils from five to fourteen were being developed in the wake of TGAT, the pre-National

Curriculum GCSE was deploying moderation methods which had their origins in practice in the public examination system prior to 1986. The requirement that coursework should be an element in the assessment of each GCSE syllabus ensured that moderation of coursework became a concern of every GCSE teacher as well as of the examining groups. Where the award of grades depended entirely on coursework assessment, its moderation necessarily became central to the actual and perceived reliability of the examination.

In the absence of a survey, comparable to Harris's 1986 study, of GCSE moderation practice across all subjects and all examining groups, among the few published sources of evidence about methods in use in the early years of GCSE are the formal scrutinies undertaken each year by the Schools Examinations and Assessment Council (SEAC). For the syllabuses in ten subjects ('mostly subjects with large entries') which were scrutinised in 1988 (SEAC, 1990), 'with one exception, coursework moderation was conducted by inspection, with schools required to send a sample of their work to an external moderator. The other method observed in the 1989 scrutiny exercise was consensus moderation, in which teachers meet to agree standards.' For a further ten subjects experiencing SEAC scrutinies in 1989:

> Most coursework moderation was conducted by postal inspection, with schools required to send a sample of their work to an external moderator. In one case, inter-school assessors visited centres to view coursework and moderators then compared the grades suggested by the school with those suggested by the inter-school assessor. In another subject, moderation was largely statistical, while in a third consensus moderation, involving six or so schools in each region, was used.
>
> (SEAC, 1991, p. 3)

Though these two scrutiny reports refer only to a sample of syllabuses in the twenty subjects covered, it would seem that moderation by inspection was the method in use in all but a relatively small minority of cases.

Buchan's study (1993), focusing on practical assessment in science and drawing on a 10 per cent sample of schools in England and Wales, refers to statistical moderation and 'postal moderation' as being the two most widely adopted methods, with the latter 'the most widely used form of moderation, operating to varying degrees throughout all the groups' (p. 175).

The examining groups themselves have also reviewed practice in coursework assessment and moderation (Joint Council for the GCSE, 1990). They list six main types of task which may be included in the internally assessed component of the examination:

- written assignments,
- investigative projects,
- problem-solving projects,
- practical assessments,
- performance tests (for example in music),
- oral tests.

In addition to statistical moderation and moderation by inspection (usually through the post), they identify moderation through the review of marking within consortia of teachers as a third category of method. The inspection of samples of candidates' work is, however, 'by far the most common' of current practices.

When making decisions on which moderation method to employ in the examining of a particular syllabus, examining groups have, subject to any requirements set out in the GCSE subject criteria, drawn on prior experience to devise schemes they judged appropriate. In those circumstances it seems probable that some of the variations noted by Harris in preferred moderation methods, across subjects and across examining groups, have persisted. For example, while the Southern Examining Group has shown interest in a model leading to moderation through accreditation of centres, the Northern Examining Association has made more use than the other groups of statistical moderation methods.

Evaluation of moderation practice

In the increasingly high-profile policy debate about coursework, referred to above, the effectiveness of moderation arrangements has not often surfaced as a specific focus of attention. Several HMI and SEAC reports on GCSE over the period 1988 to 1992 made reference to weaknesses in moderation but there have been at least as many complimentary references to moderation practice in those reports. Those references mention moderation only in very general terms and do not, for example, attempt to compare the effectiveness of different methods. Given that the experience of coursework moderation was to be found in only a minority of subjects, syllabuses and schools before 1986, it is surprising that the use of moderation methods throughout the GCSE examination system did not bring with it more obvious and more widespread problems.

It may be helpful to make a distinction between practice as viewed from what could be termed the technical perspective of those responsible for managing the examination and from the professional perspective of the teacher. As for other aspects of the procedures in external examinations (Chapter 3), little has been revealed of any evaluation of practice carried out by the examining bodies themselves. In the report from the research committee of the GCSE examining groups (Joint Council for the GCSE, 1990) no direct evidence is presented as to the effectiveness of moderation methods; the groups' experience in this respect is translated instead into 'principles of good moderation practice'.

Evidence from research into moderation from the professional perspective is also sparse but some common threads can be discerned in the conclusions of several studies. From a study of implementation of GCSE English in two local education authorities in England, Grant (1989) concluded (p. 140): 'most teachers felt that the moderation could and should have been an important and integral part of the GCSE process and it did not, ultimately, achieve this'. Daugherty *et al.* (1991), studying implementation of GCSE in Wales in three subjects (geography, history and Welsh), reported that among teachers a 'dominant theme . . . was the need to develop external moderation procedures' (p. 143): 'In the narrowest definition of the function of these procedures, some teachers would like more assurance that they do indeed serve to ensure consistency of standards. More broadly, many urged the extension of external moderation procedures so that they become more than an external control on consistency.' Buchan (1993, p. 177) concluded from her study of practical assessment in science that moderation procedures 'are seen by the teaching profession as judgemental, show little understanding of the circumstances within which they are to be implemented, and do not permit time for reflection and professional development'.

The teachers whose views are reported in these studies are not necessarily judging moderation procedures to be inadequate for the purpose of aligning standards within any one cohort of examination candidates, although suspicions about adequacy are voiced often enough for it to be fair to say that many remain to be convinced on this count. What they are saying is that, unless those procedures include training in assessment and moderation, regular feedback from moderators and direct contact between moderators and teachers, the moderation process will not be as effective as it could be. They do see a prospect of what Harlen (Chapter 1) has called 'optimum dependability' in coursework assessment backed by effective moderation, but the system they participate in is some considerable distance away from that prospect.

What those teachers are in effect articulating is a need for greater emphasis on what Wiliam (1991) has termed the 'quality assurance' side of moderation, concerned with the continuing process of arriving at fair assessments. What the examining boards are clearly operating for the most part is a system which has 'quality control', concerned with adjusting outcomes of teachers' assessment, as its main aim though it would be wrong to characterise all current moderation practice as being at the quality control end of the spectrum. One study of two examinations among the pilot sixteen-plus schemes which preceded GCSE (Daugherty, 1985) illustrates practice, in the same subject and the same examining board, at the two ends of that spectrum. Indications of moderation procedures now in use across the several syllabuses in each of the many subjects examined by the GCSE examining groups would suggest that there remains a great diversity of moderation practice. In some schemes there is external control with no training of teachers or feedback to them; others involve regular interaction between teacher and moderator throughout the assessment cycle.

Policy on GCSE coursework and moderation

While coursework moderation procedures were being designed and implemented, changes in government thinking about the GCSE were leading to the reduced emphasis on coursework referred to earlier. Policymakers have come to their own conclusions about coursework and its moderation, finding both to be, to an extent, unsatisfactory. The argument that coursework assessment was insufficiently reliable to play more than a minor role in the award of grades has gained credence and has contributed to changes in assessment and moderation practice as well as in the proportion of credit allocated to coursework. Following the questioning of GCSE 'standards' by Secretary of State, John Patten, in September 1992, SEAC's response (SEAC, 1992b) included several suggestions for tightening the grip of examining groups on coursework practice:

> The Council's view is that rather more needs to be done than HMI suggest if coursework assessment and moderation arrangements generally are to command full confidence. Recent discussions with chief moderators have helped pin-point difficulties; improvements in practice are required by SEAC's new criteria. The general criteria require groups to set coursework tasks themselves or to provide explicit criteria for task-setting. Groups are also required to provide training in task-setting, marking and standardisation. . . .
>
> Where school departments have been very lax, HMI suggest that examining groups should feel freer to take a much firmer line. SEAC sees a need for formal arrangements which operate when a school's practice is inadequate.

In effect, what was being signalled was the constraining of some of the freedoms previously enjoyed by examining groups in devising and managing schemes of coursework assessment, and by teachers in exercising their responsibilities within those frameworks. The references to examining groups setting coursework tasks themselves and to penalties for schools judged unsatisfactory point also to a tightening up in which quality control would impact upon the ways in which teachers can assess their students.

The *Mandatory Code of Practice for the GCSE* (SEAC, 1993) represents a further significant stage in the codification of practice in examining. The demands on examining bodies in respect of coursework and moderation are spelled out in statements such as:

> The examining group must set down explicit parameters, marking criteria and instructions for the setting of coursework tasks and preparation of provisional mark schemes.
>
> The examining group must specify the conditions under which coursework can take place.
>
> The examining group must provide centres with full details of the moderation procedures which apply.
>
> SEAC, 1993, pp. 16, 18)

Perhaps surprisingly, there is little attention given in all this to the relative merits of alternative methods of moderating coursework. The only reference to methods in the revised general criteria (SEAC, 1992c), which will govern all syllabuses and schemes of examining, leaves open the decision on method: 'Different kinds of coursework require different methods of moderation. The method(s) used in an examination must be fully justifiable on educational grounds and must be the most effective available, bearing in mind the need not to make unreasonable demands on resources.'

Whatever the changes in the climate of policy-making affecting decisions on the broad character of public examinations, practitioners, whether working for examining groups or as teachers assessing their students, are faced with the continuing challenge of optimising the dependability of coursework assessment. 'The usefulness of an assessment is directly related to its validity, providing it is not so low in reliability as to call this into question' (Chapter 1, p. 13). The reliability of coursework assessment and moderation in the GCSE has been called into question. If the place of coursework in public examination is to be secured for the future it would be helpful to clarify some of the dimensions relevant to constructing effective arrangements for the moderation of teachers' assessments.

Discussion

Several of the dimensions touched upon in this chapter are relevant to any rethinking of moderation practice.

The first of these is the perception of moderation as a *process* rather than as an event. In terms of the time sequence of events in an assessment, irrespective of the desired emphasis on quality assurance or quality control, events both before and after the point at which a teacher judges a student's performance on a task will impact upon the quality of assessment. The process of moderation begins with what is defined, whether in course content, assessment criteria or procedural rules, in the published syllabus and associated documents. This is the case for all types of coursework, from those which have a written outcome available for inspection to those where evidence of attainment is ephemeral. Those definitions are the starting point for a process which extends through teaching, learning and teachers' assessments to those steps formally identified as being 'moderation procedures'.

The second and third dimensions which can usefully be highlighted are those referred to earlier in the SEC Working Paper 3 (1986) as the two special features of moderation in the context of school-based assessment – the scale of the exercise and the fact that teachers are automatically assessors. The procedures affecting quality of assessment are not just several in character as they extend through the whole process from syllabus to the final award of a grade. They are also *layered*, in the sense that, for each and every syllabus, they operate at the level of the individual teacher, of the team of teachers teaching in a school, of the individual moderator, and of the team of moderators responsible for the coursework undertaken by candidates. If there is a large candidate entry the inherent complexity and layering of the process is compounded by the sheer number of people involved. At each layer in the system and at every stage of the process the procedures must operate effectively for quality to be assured. The consistency of the judgements of teachers in different schools, or within the same school, is a natural matter for concern among those who suspect undue variability. But the comparability of the judgements of the moderators in a team is just as important for the operation of this inherently complex and large-scale process.

With end-of-course examinations, those responsible for judgements are employed as examiners (though they may also be teachers) and supervised by team leaders and chief examiners. There are real problems of comparability here also (Chapter 3) but they are not usually exposed to outside scrutiny. With coursework assessment the assessors are teachers who bring to the task whatever expertise and experience they may have acquired or which may have been specifically provided, in the form of guidance and/or training, by the examining board. Their expertise in assessment is inevitably variable and is clearly a potential source of unreliability in the process. Hence the stress in recent policy pronouncements by SEAC on solutions which could involve 'prevention' in the form of training or the more drastic 'cure' of schools being disbarred from a scheme if their practice is deemed unsatisfactory.

A fourth dimension worth commenting upon is the *rule-bound* character of coursework assessment and moderation. Whereas markers of examination papers work, closely supervised, to marking schemes which indicate the credit to be given to each of a limited number of possible alternatives, coursework assessment is by definition diverse in character and carried out by teachers reaching their decisions independently of each other and of the moderators. How far can the rules about what is to be set and what is to be credited constrain those decisions without undermining the basic rationale of coursework? All the independent evidence on coursework – HMI reports, SEAC scrutinies and academic research (for example: Scott, 1991) – points to variation in the task set as a major source of inconsistency in coursework assessment. That the tasks set are not identical and the conditions for completing them are different are essential features of teachers assessing their own pupils. Indeed the justification for school-based assessments rests on taking account of attainment demonstrated in contexts other than the timed, unseen examination paper and giving teachers some freedom to determine what those contexts should be. However, unless the moderation procedures impact in some way on the type of task set and on the circumstances under which candidates complete the task, a major source of unreliability will remain.

It is the rules laid down in syllabus documentation, interpreted in any direct contact teachers have with moderators and reinterpreted in any feedback given by moderators to teachers after the event which are the basis on which standards of assessment can be aligned. More might be achieved, without any undue restriction on teachers in setting and marking their students' work, by clarifying the rules governing the setting of tasks, how they are marked and the selection of work for moderation.

But merely restating and reinterpreting the rules will not be effective if the channels of *communication* do not operate so that understanding of what is being assessed and how it can be done on a fair and consistent basis is not shared by teachers with each other and by moderators working with teachers. Buchan (1993) has argued that moderation could be more effective if teachers as internal assessors were viewed by the examining bodies as partners in working towards a shared objective of comparability of procedures and judgements, both across and within schools. Daugherty *et al.* (1991) also reported teachers as being to some extent unclear about what was expected and seeking more helpful feedback from the examining board. Their requests for clarification relate to all aspects of the coursework assessment process – setting tasks, interpreting marking criteria and operating the internal and external moderation procedures. It appears that what is presumably thought by the examining groups to be sufficient for quality control purposes as they affect a particular student cohort is often neither fully understood by teachers nor regarded as adequate for the purpose of enhancing quality assurance over time. The perceived deficiency is in part a matter of whether moderation procedures are sufficiently extensive but it is also to do with how readily and how effectively teachers and moderators communicate with each other both about the rules governing the system and about the judgements made on students' coursework.

Conclusion

The definition of moderation quoted earlier, 'the process of aligning standards of internal assessment', places the emphasis on minimising inconsistency in the standards applied by teachers in judging pupil attainment. The minimising of inconsistency depends upon both achieving a shared understanding of what is required and putting in place a means of comparing the judgements of the many teachers engaged in assessing their pupils' attainments. Some existing moderation methods focus more on achieving shared understanding through a programme of training, exemplification and feedback on practice. Consensus moderation typically emphasises the contribution it can make to reducing future differences in interpretation of the standard as well as reaching agreement on the candidates whose work is being compared. In contrast both statistical moderation and external inspection are designed mainly to check and, where necessary, amend teachers' decisions on the particular cohort of candidates whose results are being analysed and work inspected.

The case for teacher assessments remains a powerful one, with demonstrable gains in validity, strongly supported by all those, politicians and professionals, who advocated it as a fundamental feature of the GCSE. But that case has been clouded subsequently by questioning, some of it ideologically motivated but some of it also coming from a more pragmatic view of the GCSE experience, of the reliability of assessment of coursework and the associated adequacy of moderation procedures. Reliability can only be a matter of optimum dependability and there are clearly resource constraints involved. But any form of assessment leading to certification cannot be so low in reliability that its validity is seriously called into question.

References

Buchan, A. (1993) Policy into practice: internal assessment at 16+, standardization and moderation procedures, *Education Research*, Vol. 35, no. 2, pp. 171–9.

Cohen, L. and Deale, R. N. (1977) *Assessment by Teachers in Examinations at 16+*, Schools Council Examination Bulletin 37, Evans/ Methuen Educational, London.

Daugherty, R. (1985) *Examining Geography at 16+*, Secondary Examinations Council, London.

Daugherty, R. Thomas, B., Jones, G. E. and Davies, S. (1991) *GCSE in Wales*, Welsh Office Education Department, Cardiff.

DES/WO (Department of Education and Science/Welsh Office) (1985a) *Better Schools*, Department of Education and Science/Welsh Office, London.

DES/WO (1985b) *General Certificate of Secondary Education: The National Criteria*, Department of Education and Science/Welsh Office, London.

DES/WO (1988) *The Task Group on Assessment and Testing: A Report*, Department of Education and Science/Welsh Office, London.

Goldstein, H. (1986) Models for equating test scores and for studying comparability in public examinations, in D. L. Nuttall (ed.) *Assessing Educational Achievement*, Falmer Press, Lewes.

Grant, M. (1989) *GCSE in Practice*, NFER-Nelson, Windsor.

Harris, A. (1986) *School-Based Assessment in GCE and CSE Boards: A Report on Policy and Practice*, Secondary Examinations Council, London.

Hillgate Group (1987) *The Reform of British Education*, The Claridge Press, London.

HMI (Her Majesty's Inspectorate) (1988) *The Introduction of the General Certificate of Secondary Education in Schools, 1986–88*, Department of Education and Science, London.

Joint Council for the GCSE: Inter-Group Research Committee (1990) *Good Practice in Assessing and Moderating Centre-Assessed Components of GCSE Examinations*, Joint Council for the GCSE.

Kingdon, M. and Stobart, G. (1988) *GCSE Examined*, Falmer Press, London.

North, J. (ed.) (1987) *The GCSE: An Examination*, The Claridge Press, London.

Nuttall, D. L. and Thomas, S. (1993) *Monitoring Procedures Based on Centre Performance Variables*, Research and Development Series No. 11, Training, Enterprise and Education Directorate, Sheffield.

Schools Council (1965) *The Certificate of Secondary Education: School-Based Examinations*, Schools Council, London.

Scott, D. (1991) Issues and themes: coursework and coursework assessment in the GCSE, *Research Papers in Education*, Vol. 6, no. 1, pp. 3–19.

SEAC (School Examination and Assessment Council) (1990) *Examining GCSE: First General Scrutiny Report*, School Examination and Assessment Council, London.

SEAC (1991) *Examining GCSE: Second General Scrutiny Report*, School Examination and Assessment Council, London.

SEAC (1992a) *GCSE/Key Stage 4 Standards for Assessment and Certification: Glossary of Terms*, School Examination and Assessment Council, London.

SEAC (1992b) *GCSE Examinations Quality and Standards: Advice to the Secretary of State*, School Examination and Assessment Council, London.

SEAC (1992c) *GCSE/Key Stage 4 Standards for Assessment and Certification: General Criteria*, School Examination and Assessment Council, London.

SEAC (1993) *Mandatory Code of Practice for the GCSE*, School Examination and Assessment Council, London.

SEC (Secondary Examinations Council) (1985) *Coursework Assessment in GCSE* (Working Paper 2), Secondary Examinations Council, London.

SEC (1986) *Policy and Practice in School-Based Assessment* (Working Paper 3), Secondary Examinations Council, London.

Wiliam, D. (1992) Some technical issues in assessment: a user's guide, *British Journal of Curriculum and Assessment*, Vol. 2, no. 3, pp. 11–20.

7

EXPERIENCE OF QUALITY ASSURANCE AT KEY STAGE 1

Mary James

Introduction

This chapter develops some of the quality assurance themes introduced in earlier chapters, particularly those by Harlen and Gipps, by exploring experience of moderation and audit in the context of National Curriculum Assessment (NCA) in England and Wales during the period from the publication of the report of the Task Group on Assessment and Testing (DES/WO, 1988a) to the publication of the final report of the government-commissioned review of National Curriculum and assessment carried out by Sir Ron Dearing in 1993 (Dearing, 1994). For reasons partly to do with the phased introduction of the National Curriculum, partly to do with the different characteristics of education at the various Key Stages, and partly, one suspects, for political reasons, the quality assurance structures and procedures that had been tried out by the time of the Dearing Review exhibited considerable differences across Key Stages. At Key Stage 1 (KS1) a system of 'moderation' involving teams of visiting moderators appointed by local education authorities (LEAs), backed up by local assessment training, was established in 1991. At KS3, however, a very different system of 'quality audit' was introduced in 1992, though it was effectively 'put on hold' by the teachers' boycott in 1993. 'Quality audit' required schools to send samples of test scripts and other evidence of assessments to GCSE examining groups, as designated audit agencies, for 'audit' and

Copyright © 1994, Mary James

'endorsement'. By the beginning of 1994 the issue of moderation or audit at KS2 had still to be resolved and the Dearing Report (1994) recommended no decision until the new School Curriculum and Assessment Authority (SCAA) had carried out a further review of the options.

Thus the most extensive experience of quality assurance procedures in relation to NCA was, by the end of 1993, to be found in KS1 infants' schools and classrooms. Therefore, although quality assurance in NCA is the general context, this chapter takes as its particular focus an examination of the accumulating evidence of experience at Key Stage 1. In this sense it is a specific case study of KS1 nested within the broader case of NCA. But it is more specific still, because the themes and issues discussed have particular reference to evidence from schools and LEAs in the East Anglian region of England between 1990 and 1993. Whilst this might seem to locate it within a specific time and place, the issues raised have much general interest and relevance to the themes of this book. These studies are the only independent research specifically concerned with moderation practice in the National Curriculum, available at the current time. Remarkably, given the concern for quality in assessment, this area has even been neglected by Her Majesty's Inspectors (HMI). Their report on assessment, recording and reporting at Key Stages 1, 2 and 3 for 1992/3 had only very mixed and inconclusive observations to offer on quality control and the audit process based on 'some second-hand evidence'!

> The audit process was not formally inspected this year, but HMI obtained some second-hand evidence through discussions with teachers. The extent and quality of the audit process appeared to be uneven. Many schools had visits of varying duration and it appears that different auditors interpreted their duties differently. For some schools, it was apparent that the audit involved careful scrutiny of a selection of pupils' standard tasks and teacher-assessed work. Evidence from other teachers indicated that the audit consisted of a brief discussion of how things had gone, a look at the pupils' results and a query from the auditor as to whether there were any problems. If the audit process is to continue, there is a need for more consistency of approach.
>
> (HMI, 1994, para. 12)

The evidence available from our studies is much more robust than this and leads us to somewhat different conclusions, notably that, although substantial problems remain, schools and local authorities in the East Anglian region, at least, are moving towards greater consistency of approach.

In order to put these findings into perspective, this chapter begins with a short description of the research which informs it. This is followed by a brief resumé of relevant elements of national policy and a discussion of the assumptions inherent in central arrangements and requirements for assessment and moderation. The responses of a group of six LEAs to the obligations placed upon them is then outlined, followed by an account of the implementation of policy in schools and some of the issues that have arisen at the level of practice. Throughout, special attention is given to dilemmas that arise from demands that exceed the available resource: how to meet needs for both specificity and comprehensiveness in the assessment training of teachers and moderators; how to marry the functions of audit and support in the role of the moderator; how to meet the dual criteria for validity and reliability of assessments and how to determine whose is the responsibility for each; how to balance accountability and development purposes and associated mechanisms for quality control on the one hand and quality assurance on the other. Some explanations for what emerges are offered in relation to the influence of existing professional cultures in the development of strategies for assuring assessment quality. Consequently, the attempt to introduce new systems is equivalent to bringing about cultural change and must, therefore, be framed according to a timescale and with attention to the human dimensions that cultural change entails. To regard putting in place a quality assurance system as little more than a technical or bureaucratic exercise involving the design of structures, the delineation of roles and the distribution of resources is to court the kind of reaction that led to the teachers' boycott in 1993.

Finally, the proposals for future moderation of national assessment, outlined in Sir Ron Dearing's interim and final reports, are explored. In terms of TGAT's original classification of moderation options, three years' experience and a national review appear to have done little to provide a clear way forward and the confusion continues to be rooted in a tension between quality assurance of assessment processes and quality control of assessment results. The chapter concludes with a discussion of the possibility of incorporating a greater degree of quality control within quality assurance systems with the twin aims of supporting professional and educational developments and gaining the confidence of a sceptical wider community in assessment outcomes.

The research

The following description and analysis of experience in schools and LEAs is based largely on the outcomes of three linked evaluation projects carried out at the University of Cambridge Institute of Education, on behalf of LEAs in East Anglia from 1990. The first study was an evaluation of KS1 assessment training in Bedfordshire LEA in 1990/1 during the first (supposedly 'unreported') run of NCA in the core subjects (English, mathematics and science) for all children in Year 2. The research involved observation of assessment training sessions and the conduct of the 1991 assessments in schools supported by interviews with LEA advisers, moderators and teachers. The results of this study were written up in a report to the LEA (Conner and James, 1991).

The second study involved four LEAs (Essex, Hertfordshire, Norfolk and Suffolk) and focused specifically on moderation and the obligation placed upon LEAs by the then School Examination and Assessment Council (SEAC) to promote consistent standards of assessment within and across LEAs. The data were again collected through observation of training sessions but also by 'shadowing' moderators as they carried out their tasks. Accompanying moderators on their visits to schools also provided opportunities to observe and talk with teachers. The outcomes of this study were made available in the form of a report to the LEAs (James and Conner, 1992) and a journal article (James and Conner, 1993).

The third study continued to monitor assessment practice in schools and LEAs in the light of the 1992/3 Assessment Order for KS1 and to extend the analyses generated by the research undertaken in 1991/2. This time, however, the group of LEAs was extended to six (Bedfordshire, Cambridgeshire, Essex, Hertfordshire, Norfolk and Suffolk). In order to counteract any bias that might have been introduced in the earlier study by shadowing moderators and taking LEA arrangements as a starting point, a decision was taken to make case studies of schools (two or three schools in each LEA) the primary focus of this research. This change in approach was also a response to the shift in emphasis introduced by the Department for Education (DfE Circular 12/92) which gave headteachers a statutory duty to see that their school's assessment standards conformed to national standards. The report of this study was presented to the LEAs at the end of September 1993 (Conner and James, 1993).

The national policy context

On the basis of the TGAT Report (DES/WO 1988a) the then Department of Education and Science (DES) began to put in place a national assessment system with the following espoused characteristics:

• serving several purposes – formative, diagnostic, summative and evaluative;

- combining moderated teacher assessment (TA) with standard assessment tasks or tests (SATs);
- aggregated and reported at the end of Key Stages – at the ages of seven, eleven, fourteen and sixteen;
- criterion-referenced – in relation to attainment targets (ATs);
- based on a progressive ten-level scale for attainment in each of the subjects with Level 1 being the lowest.

TGAT recognised many of the difficulties inherent in relation to each of these dimensions but managed to persuade the Secretary of State that this was a viable framework in all but one respect – moderation. In devoting four pages of its main report to the issue, TGAT recognised the importance of quality assurance in assessment and saw moderation as having a key role in this. Moderation, according to TGAT, had twin functions: 'to communicate general standards to individual assessors and to control aberrations from general standards by appropriate adjustments' (DES/WO, 1988a, para. 68). In other words, both a training function and an audit function were recognised at this early stage. TGAT went on to examine the options before making a judgement about the most appropriate system of moderation for national assessment. It outlined the pros and cons of reference tests, moderation by inspection and group moderation before recommending the latter on the basis of its 'communication' potential to enhance the professional judgement of teachers and to allow their judgements to inform the development of the National Curriculum (see also Chapter 4).

In view of what has happened subsequently it is worth going back to the TGAT Report to look at what was said about each of these alternatives. With respect to reference tests, it was thought that SATs could be used as reference tests against which to scale teachers' ratings. This would be economical but it would require the tests to reflect precisely the same features as the teachers' ratings and would almost inevitably encourage 'teaching to the test' since the test alone would determine the level of reported attainment. Moderation by inspection would similarly emphasise external control and would suffer from incompleteness of data because visiting moderators usually have access only to tangible outcomes of tasks, or processes by special arrangements which can introduce an element of artificialty. TGAT's preferred group moderation, based on practice in GCE and CSE examinations at sixteen-plus, emphasised the development of collective judgement through discussion and exchange of samples of children's work at meetings. The 'pattern-matching technique' described by TGAT in some detail emphasised the function of the moderation meetings as scrutinising differences between teacher ratings and scores on standard tasks (STs) and between the distribution of pupils' scores in a class or school with LEA and national distributions. 'The general aim would be to adjust the overall teacher rating results to match the overall results of the national tests' (DES/WO, 1988a, para. 74) unless there was a good reason not to do so in which case these reasons would be reported to the LEA and to SEAC. This almost exclusive emphasis on harmonising school results with national distributions is curious, given the commitment to criterion-referencing, although it is understandable because the only existing experience was with norm-referenced systems. Little attention at this time was given to the function of group moderation in interpreting criteria and in establishing the kind of performance that would count as demonstration of attainment, although the TGAT supplementary reports (DES/WO, 1988b, p. 5) mentioned the use of assessed tasks to serve as national standards. Of course, the moment it proposed a ten-level scale, with expectations that, for instance, the majority of seven-year-olds would attain Level 2, a normative dimension was introduced, which supports the view that you only have to scratch the surface of criterion-referenced assessment to find norm-referenced assessment lurking beneath (Angoff, 1974, cited in Wiliam, 1993; Black, Harlen and Orgee, 1984).

In June 1988, when announcing his acceptance of most of the TGAT Report, the Secretary of State specifically rejected TGAT's recommendations for moderation on the basis that they were too 'complicated and costly' and that there was insufficient control to 'safeguard standards'. According to Daugherty (1994, Chapter 4), ministers adopted the convenient tactic of 'wait and see what emerges from developments' because they had no coherent alternative to offer at this time. It therefore fell to SEAC to come up with something different. In 1989 it proposed a model for the moderation of KS1 assessment, with which it was most concerned at the time, based on the establishment of local moderating groups (though not groups of teachers as TGAT had proposed). These would receive and compare TA and ST scores although ST scores were to be 'preferred' for reporting purposes. If a teacher queried the ST score then a local moderation procedure (which became known as 'reconciliation') would be invoked probably involving an external moderator who would visit schools to look at the evidence. Not surprisingly, since it is difficult to imagine who else might possess the structures, experience and personnel needed to work with up to 20,000 infants' and primary schools, SEAC proposed that local education authorities should manage the local moderating groups and appoint local moderators. Daugherty notes that, in this 'rather different method', group moderation by teachers had effectively been replaced by 'moderation by inspection'. He also claims that the greatest significance in these new proposals should be attached to the shift away from TGAT's conception of moderation as a professional process of teacher and curriculum development, as well as control, towards moderation as an administrative process concerned primarily with bureaucratic regulation of assessment practices. Groups of teachers meeting together still figured in SEAC's plans but these were to have a role in training teachers for national assessment and agreement trialling.

Understandably, given its growing interest in reducing the role and power of the LEAs, the DES was cautious in its acceptance of SEAC's model but, since no other feasible alternative readily presented itself, these proposals became the basis of the moderation system that has subsequently evolved for KS1.

Before moving on to examine the ways in which LEAs responded to the obligations placed upon them, it is perhaps worth pausing to reflect upon some of the unanswered questions and assumptions that were inherent in the proposals being made at national level. These are important because they foreshadow some of the issues that emerged forcefully in the process of implementation at local level. Firstly, the relationship between teacher assessment and ST assessment and the relationship of both to the acknowledged purposes of national assessment was left unarticulated. Secondly, the validity and reliability of the STs, to be produced by commissioned test development agencies, appeared to be regarded as unproblematic so no mention was specifically made of the need to moderate the STs themselves. Thirdly, it was assumed that LEAs, many of which had previously seen their role primarily as supporting development in schools, would be willing and equipped to take on 'quality control' in assessment and combine it in some way with their training programmes. Fourthly, it was left unclear how the moderation decisions made in one LEA would be made consistent with those made in other LEAs although it was assumed that SEAC would be the 'linchpin' and provide some national training and materials for use in agreement trialling. And finally, it was assumed that effective moderation could be provided on a fairly limited – and reducing – budget.

Arrangements at LEA level

In response to a sequence of directives from the DES and SEAC setting out their responsibilities and inviting their bids for grants for education support and training (GEST), LEAs began to set up their moderating groups (often their 'assessment teams' headed by an inspector or adviser for assessment) and to appoint local moderators. Hundreds of moderators were needed because the focus of their work was rapidly redefined to include the moderation of the STs which were to be administered and marked by teachers in a limited time period during Year 2. If all schools were to receive two or three visits around this period, no moderator could be expected to cover more than about ten to fifteen schools. Hence the need for large numbers of moderators. Understandably LEAs found it difficult to identify suitable people. In the East Anglian region a variety of arrangements were made. One LEA used its own advisers and advisory teachers exclusively. Another appointed head-teachers and deputy headteachers for one year but abandoned this tactic when many had to relinguish their commitment because of career moves or in-school emergencies. A third LEA appointed a variety of people who were regarded as having the requisite qualities, ranging from LEA advisory staff to seconded teachers and 'bought in' lecturers from higher education. Who was available depended to a considerable extent on another feature of government policy during this period. Through that aspect of the Education Reform Act 1988 dealing with local financial management (LMS), and the subsequent Education (Schools) Act 1993, LEAs were left in little doubt that the government intended that the maximum funds and responsibility should eventually be devolved to schools. There was evidence that LEAs responded in different ways to this. Within East Anglia, one LEA, a pioneer in the field of LMS, devolved as much as possible to schools as early as possible and set up self-financing agencies so that schools could 'buy back' services as required. Another LEA retained its central funds as long as possible. The latter therefore was in a better position than the former to support a substantial team of advisers and advisory teachers who might take on the roles of moderators. All this goes to show that at the point of implementation it is rarely possible to examine elements of policy in isolation because one area (e.g. assessment policy) is inevitably affected by others (e.g. funding policy).

In its 1989 recommendation that LEAs should administer assessment arrangements, SEAC deliberately sought to link quality control with assessment training by setting out the pattern of a three-phase 'assessment cycle' (Daugherty, 1994). Despite the fact that teacher assessment was supposed to cover the whole of the Key Stage, this was associated in SEAC's collective mind with Year 2. The first phase, in the first two terms of Year 2, would involve assessment training of teachers including 'agreement trials' in which teachers would align their judgements of children's work. The second phase would be the ST period, which, until 1993, was confined to the first half of the summer term. This would then be followed by the third phase in which teacher assessments and ST scores would be reconciled and results confirmed. It was envisaged that local moderators would have a role in each of these phases. Indeed, the 1991 *Moderator's Handbook*, issued by SEAC, described moderators' duties in terms of: planning and providing training for teachers; supporting and advising during assessment; resolving differences between ST and TA results; promoting consistency of standards; evaluating the effectiveness of the assessment cycle. Our evidence suggests that this multiplicity of roles has been a source of difficulty both to the moderators themselves and to the teachers with whom they have worked because there have been clashes of expectation particularly in relation to the balance of support and audit functions.

In the period since 1989 some modifications to the assessment model have been made, most notably: the ST period has been extended to reduce the pressure on Year 2 teachers; TA scores have no longer to be submitted before the STs are completed and therefore can take the latter into account; and the emphasis in moderation has shifted towards the quality control function of 'audit'. Progressive changes in arrangements for funding in-service courses for teachers have also tended to undermine SEAC's original rationale by effectively separating training from audit in terms of funding. In future, LEAs may 'offer' training in curriculum and assessment but decisions about whether it is taken up will rest wholly with the schools thus making consistency in assessment practice even more difficult to achieve.

From the beginning, LEAs received very little specific guidance on how to go about the task of assuring quality in assessments within and between schools and within and between LEAs. They were just told that this was expected of them. In the *Moderator's Handbook* (SEAC, 1991), for instance, they were informed that:

> An aspect of moderation that will certainly grow in importance is the promotion of consistent standards of assessment, both within the LEA and also, gradually, across the country as a whole.
> (SEAC, 1991, para. 6)

> Because consistency of approach and of standards needs to be developed across the country as a whole, and not just separately within each LEA, LEAs are required by the GEST arrangements for 1992/3 to say in their National Curriculum plans how they intend to promote consistency of assessment standards between their own schools and those in other LEAs.
> (SEAC, 1991, para. 53)

Thus the onus for creating a system of quality assurance seemed to be thrown on to the shoulders of the LEAs at a time when their power and influence over schools was being reduced and when they were, through, for example, the 1991 publication of league tables of LEA results, being encouraged to compete with one another rather than to work collaboratively.

Within the East Anglian region, LEAs recognised 'strength in unity' and decided to take seriously the instruction to develop plans to promote intra- and inter-LEA consistency. A regional group of the national Association of Inspectors and Advisers for Assessment (AIAA) met regularly at the Cambridge Institute of Education, to which the researchers were invited first as 'critical friends' then as members. This small group of senior assessment advisers/inspectors in each of the six counties shared their interpretations of central directives, as they emerged from government and SEAC, and their local plans and materials for assessment training and audit. Thus a good deal of cross-fertilisation was encouraged. They also decided to link up in other tangible ways. In particular they arranged inter-LEA agreement trials involving their assessment teams and paired moderation visits across LEA boundaries. The joint agreement trials were considered to be successful, and are continuing on a regular basis, although the paired moderation meetings proved difficult to arrange because of the already hectic schedules of moderators. Another aspect of collaboration was, of course, the joint funding of the research projects described here, the reports of which were used to inform LEA bids for in-service funds and the development of training materials for moderation.

As a result of these contacts over the years a similar pattern of moderation was beginning to emerge although there was still scope for considerable local variation. To some extent it built on the original SEAC three-phase assessment cycle but with some interesting differences in emphasis. The first phase, the training phase, received great attention in the first two years of national assessment (1991 and 1992) and LEAs were concerned that this training should not be limited to Year 2 teachers in relation to the STs. Taking on board issues of consistency and continuity across years, and even Key Stages, they tried to involve all teachers in the school. In 1991 one authority even managed to insist that all primary teachers should receive assessment training. LEAs also defined broadly the scope of training and, although some of this was concerned with agreement trialling in relation to specific STs and TAs, they also ran sessions on integrating assessments into the curriculum and on the development of whole-school assessment policy and practice. In so far as not everything that might be relevant could be covered in the limited time that individuals had available for training, some selection had to be made either by the providers or by the recipients of training.

Since there was no guarantee that all teachers had received the same training some inconsistencies in practice were almost inevitable. Most LEAs were well aware of this but chose to encourage the development of practices that would contribute to quality assurance in the longer term rather than concentrate on the impossible task of standardising judgements on all the hundreds of statements of attainment that had now become the assessment criteria for determining the levels achieved on the attainment targets.

In the first years of national assessment, moderators were involved, to a greater or lesser extent, in the assessment training of the teachers in the schools to which they were allocated, although this arrangement began to fall away as moderators were brought in from schools on limited contracts. Moderators had themselves to be trained in the specific tasks assigned to them and by 1993 the usual training period was two to three days. In these training days they worked together on developing common judgements through agreement trials using both local materials and those that had been distributed by SEAC at national conferences and through the series of SEAC publications called *Children's Work Assessed*. But there was also much to learn about the process of reconciliation, about provision for children with special educational needs, about how to deal with the paper work and the optical mark reader sheets, etc. It was therefore unlikely that the time available would be sufficient for all moderators to acquire a uniform approach to their tasks and a consistent set of judgements. Moreover, there was the added complication of the varied backgrounds and motivations that moderators brought with them to the work. In our third study (Conner and James, 1993) there was considerable evidence that moderators who shared the same training still came away with different interpretations of what was expected of them. In perhaps the most extreme example, one moderator saw himself at the 'quality assurance' end, promoting good assessment practice in schools with no real authority to change teachers' judgements, whereas another moderator in the same authority wanted to give the audit process 'teeth' by insisting on common approaches to assessment tasks across schools.

LEAs recognised that many questions would arise after the formal training phase so most established 'helplines' which proved invaluable to both teachers and moderators. The moderation period itself (roughly equivalent to SEAC's second and third phases of the assessment cycle) had, by 1993, also settled down into a recognisable pattern across East Anglian LEAs. Most moderators were responsible for approximately ten schools (though considerably more in one authority) and were expected to make two or three visits to each school within and around the

ST period. Typically the first visit was used to make contact and to talk with the headteacher, the school assessment leader (if appropriate) and Year 2 teachers about general assessment policy and practice in the school and to make arrangements for future visits. The second visit was usually the main visit and in these moderators mostly asked to see the conduct of one ST by each of the Year 2 teachers and their teacher assessments for a specified number of children (usually one to three). In order to scrutinise teacher assessments they asked to see tangible evidence of attainment in the form of portfolios, work books or the teacher's observational notes. The third visit would be used to complete any tasks left undone in the main visit and to deal with issues of reconciliation, confirmation and the recording of results. In an effort to ensure that children were not disadvantaged by the limited expectations of some teachers, an additional statutory duty had been placed on moderators in 1993 to ensure that children who had attained one level were given opportunities to tackle the next. So some moderators used this third visit to see teachers taking children on to the next level in their ST assessments. This did not go down too well in some schools where teachers were anxious about the psychological impact that failure at the next level would have on children.

In so far as this pattern of moderation was emerging across LEAs one could argue a case, contrary to that of HMI (1994), for convergence of practice and hence growing consistency in both the approach to assessment tasks and in the interpretation of national standards. Nevertheless, although our evidence suggests that these assumptions are broadly warranted, we also have plenty of evidence that warns us to guard against complacency. There was still plenty of scope for local variation within the similar patterns that were emerging. Most significant perhaps were differences in the relative emphasis given to quality control as opposed to quality assurance in different LEAs. The most obvious evidence of this was in the moderation reports that moderators were required to complete for the LEA and the school. In one authority this was written on a pro forma of two sides of paper under headings requesting general information about whole school policy, consistency, evidence and action planning. Most of the questions under each of these headings sought information about strategies, planning and training and indicated a concern with developments and procedures from which one might expect good assessment practice to emerge. The approach was therefore principally in the realm of 'quality assurance'. Another LEA, however, appeared to place most of its emphasis on 'quality control' by requiring moderators to complete a thirteen-page visit pro forma detailing the outcomes of specific judgements on all assessed attainment targets in the core subjects, though not, mercifully, for all children. There was other evidence that both LEAs were concerned to promote both quality assurance and quality control but there were undoubted differences in balance and emphasis.

Despite the best efforts of the LEAs, the scope and demands of national assessment have been so large, the backgrounds and qualities of moderators so diverse, and the character of the numerous schools and LEAs so varied, that the kind of control needed to assure assessment quality, in any absolute sense, has been well nigh impossible. Many of the key issues in quality assurance in national assessment at KS1 have arisen in the aforegoing discussion but they are sharpened up and added to by an examination of moderation experience in schools, which I move on to next.

Experience in schools

This section draws exclusively on the three research projects conducted since 1990 in the East Anglian region. The reports of those projects contain extensive case study material. Here, however, the discussion is organised principally around the general themes, issues and dilemmas that the case material illustrates.

From the perspective of most schools, consistency of judgements with national standards was, initially at least, of lesser interest than the need to be fair to the children and to promote their learning. Schools inevitably had a very local perspective sometimes not extending even to the LEA, let alone the nation. Whilst some teachers have in the course of time revised their perspectives, particularly after the school has received children from elsewhere with assessed levels with which they disagree, or when middle-class parents have put pressure on them to achieve quantities of Level 3s, they have remained first and foremost teachers, not examiners. Therefore inter-LEA consistency has not really been 'their' issue, which some might see as unfortunate since the administration and marking of national assessments has depended on them. Their stated interests have been primarily in the area of formative and diagnostic assessment (the first two of TGAT's purposes) for its potential to assist them with their teaching (although the teachers' conceptions of formative assessment were mostly unsophisticated and articulated more with curriculum coverage than with any coherent theory of how children learn and how assessment might contribute, as described in Chapter 4, p. 76). Despite these espoused interests, they have, however, been constrained to concentrate on the summative elements by the sheer scope of the STs and the complexity of the recording system. Consequently our evidence suggests that Year 2 teachers were in two minds about the 1993 teachers' boycott and the Dearing Review that it stimulated. On the one hand they wanted a simpler system; on the other hand and they recognised that they had learned a great deal about assessment and they did not want all their new learning to be devalued or lost.

Over the three years covered by our studies we have witnessed a shift in focus from an almost exclusive concern with the mechanisms of administering the STs and recording results towards wider concerns associated with teacher assessment, the collection of evidence, the sharing of judgements and whole school policy. I have little doubt that this is attributable to the influence and training provided by the LEAs. On the other hand the STs still feature largely and dominate the thinking and practice of teachers in the latter half of Year 2. Some teachers have said that they have learned things about their children from the STs but, in our experience, most have felt that STs merely confirmed what they already knew. Thus the formative potential of this aspect of national assessment has been limited. This is as might be expected because early on in the development of the system the roles of ST and TA appeared to become separated with SEAC ascribing the formative purpose to teacher assessment and the summative purpose to STs.

Although many of the public statements from central agencies implied that the STs themselves were unproblematic (see above), teachers and moderators have been much exercised by issues of validity and reliability arising from them, although they rarely used these terms themselves. For this reason much of the moderation effort, within schools in agreement trials and by the external moderator, has been directed towards moderating the STs. (In TGAT's proposals it was the teacher assessments, not the STs, that were expected to require moderation!) Reliability has been threatened in two particular ways: by the scope available for variations in the presentation of tasks and by the scope for interpreting the assessment criteria in different ways.

As far as consistency in the presentation of tasks was concerned we observed variation in the interpretation by teachers of the guidance offered by SEAC and the LEAs, variation in the presentation of tasks between teachers and schools and variation by some teachers in the mode of presentation from one group or individual child to another. In the 1992 study we noticed a teacher changing the format of her presentation in the light of her experience of using the material and as a result of the responses of the children. She said, 'I usually get the hang of it by the third time I've done it, after that it gets boring. . . . I don't know if it affects the children's reactions.' In 1993, when many of the STs came in a 'pencil-and-paper' format, the scope for such variation should have been reduced but, as one teacher pointed out, the options available to administer the tests either to groups or individuals probably advantaged or disadvantaged different children in different ways.

Problems about reliability in terms of consistent application of criteria for judgements of attainment were also evident. These stemmed chiefly from the scope for interpretation in the statements of attainment. For example, 'spell correctly, in the course of their own writing, simple monosyllabic words they use regularly which observe common patterns' (English: spelling: Level 2) permitted a range of interpretation around the qualifiers 'own', 'simple', 'regularly' and 'common' (see also Wiliam, 1993). Some of these problems could have been overcome if criteria had been clarified in such a way as to make them unambiguous. However, to do this in the context of the National Curriculum attainment targets would either have led to a vast increase in the already too numerous statements of attainment or to trivialisation of the learning tasks (see also Chapter 1). Some revision of the statements of attainment by SEAC during the period 1991 to 1993 indicated that it was grappling with this issue but the solution that it came up with at that time appeared to rest on selected criteria which would be key to the judgements about whether a child had achieved a particular level in key attainment targets. Thus whether or not a child had been 'told' less than eight words in a 100-word passage became critical to attainment of Level 2 in reading; similarly, whether or not a child had punctuated two sentences with full stops and capital letters became critical to attainment of Level 2 in writing. Whilst these reasonably unambiguous criteria undoubtedly enhanced the reliability of teachers' judgements on the STs, teachers were unhappy about what this did to the validity of assessments, which they articulated in terms of 'fairness' to children.

If one takes the example of the writing attainment target, many teachers and moderators encountered examples of children's writing that fulfilled all the other stated criteria concerning story structure, the sequencing of events and the introduction of characters – also some criteria that were not required at Level 2, concerning the quality of ideas and the use of vocabulary – yet these children could not be assessed as Level 2 because they had not used punctuation as required. This seemed 'unfair' especially when children could read their stories with intonation that indicated an understanding of sentences. What teachers were querying was the conception of 'writing' as defined by the criteria. In other words they were questioning the 'construct validity' of the assessment. Feeling that they were not in a position to influence changes in the definition of criteria, a certain amount of 'teaching to the test' was inevitable; evidence for this in 1993 was provided by the appearance in children's writing of full stops of golfball proportions.

Although some of these problems seemed little nearer resolution than they were four years earlier, the fact that teachers were aware of them says something about the way in which their understanding of assessment had increased. This is all the more significant in that infants' teachers, unlike secondary teachers, had very little experience with formal assessment before the introduction of national assessment. Year 2 teachers may now be among the most sophisticated assessment practitioners. There is evidence that this understanding is, at last, transferring from an obsession with STs to a consideration of teacher assessment in general and to school assessment policy in particular. It would be wrong to suggest that development is uniform across all schools (our evidence suggests that schools are still at very different stages in understanding and practice depending on development priorities within the schools and commitment to assessment by senior managers). However, in East Anglian schools, development appears to be happening in certain directions encouraged by the LEAs. As with the pattern of moderation (see above) a number of common features are becoming evident.

Firstly, there is increasing recognition of the need to collect evidence of children's performance in order to support judgements. The tick-lists of statements of attainment that so characterised the early forms of record-keeping, though not entirely supplanted, are being supplemented or replaced by portfolios of work for individual children. Teachers are still anxious about the amount of evidence they need to collect but LEAs have mostly recommended a slim portfolio containing a limited number of fully annotated pieces of evidence (perhaps one for each attainment target) to illustrate that the processes of assessment have been carried out competently and to provide material for discussion of judgements in agreement trials and with parents.

Secondly, whether or not they can be described as agreement trials, teachers have begun to meet more regularly for debate about judgements in relation to children's work. These meetings occurred within schools but also, sometimes, across schools in school cluster meetings or in LEA training. Despite growing familiarity with this kind of procedure teachers nevertheless experienced difficulty in challenging the judgements of others. In giving an account of such a meeting, one teacher said: 'Nobody wanted to say that they disagreed, especially when they thought that one of their colleagues has assessed too highly. Teachers aren't like that are they?' The reasons for this difficulty therefore appear to be cultural. Teachers are easily threatened, especially at the present moment in history, and avoid situations that make them more vulnerable. Acceptance of the need for critical examination of judgement in a public forum will entail a certain amount of cultural change which inevitably takes time.

Thirdly, in order to provide some consistency in the tasks presented to children and to focus their discussions of standards, teachers were beginning to create resource banks of assessment tasks, including some of the 'better' STs, to use as a normal part of their teaching and learning and as a basis for some of their teacher assessments.

Fourthly, in addition to individual portfolios, schools were being encouraged by LEAs to develop school portfolios of evidence of children's work agreed at the various levels. These would relate both to the material produced by SEAC, entitled *Children's Work Assessed*, and to equivalent collections that were being put together at LEA level. These portfolios act as a reference for teachers but also as a way of communicating standards to parents. By comparing their own child's work with the school portfolio parents are able to draw conclusions about the progress their child is making.

Together these components of emerging practice at school level, with the addition of school visits by external moderators to support schools in the process of making their judgements and to contribute to the developments of consistent approaches, might form the basis of a viable quality assurance system. The question is whether it would satisfy the demands for accountability at national level and from the wider community. In a letter to us (dated 29 July 1993) in response to our sending him a copy of the interim report of our 1993 study, Sir Ron Dearing indicated that a professional quality assurance model, on its own, would probably be insufficient:

> I was interested to read your reference to tension between support for a professional model of quality assurance and a bureaucratic model of quality control. I agree with you that polarisation of this kind is too stark. Quality assurance is a highly desirable approach, but it is far from easy to achieve across the totality of a system as huge and as diverse as schools, and from what I have experienced elsewhere, it does not dispose of the need for an element of quality control to verify that the systems of quality assurance are delivering acceptable standards.
>
> (Dearing, 1993a)

The implications of the Dearing Review

In April 1993 Sir Ron Dearing, the appointed Chair of the new body SCAA, was asked by John Patten, the Secretary of State, to conduct an urgent review of the National Curriculum and its assessment. In July he presented an interim report (Dearing, 1993b) and in December a final report (Dearing, 1994). Both were accepted by government in their entirety and there was much in both reports that was well received by policy-makers and professionals alike. However, the proposals for promoting quality in national assessment were interesting, not least because of the substantive differences between the two reports and the questions left unanswered – or even unasked.

There was in Dearing's proposals no suggestion that national tests (STs) should be dispensed with but that they should be limited to the core subjects of English and mathematics at KS1, at least in 1994, with less time apportioned to them. According to the interim report, they should also be slimmed down by reducing any diagnostic and formative element that they presently contain (Dearing, 1993b, para. 5.23). On a number of occasions, Dearing stated that the national tests are to be exclusively summative and teacher assessment principally formative although teacher assessment can be expected to contribute to summative assessment in science at the end of KS1 and to other summative assessments at other points in a Key Stage. However, Dearing was also concerned that teacher assessment should have 'equal standing' with national tests and recommended that the two sets of ratings 'should be shown separately in all forms of reporting and in school prospectuses' (Dearing, 1993b, para. 5.28). This suggests that teacher assessment will, in a significant way, have a summative purpose even at the ends of Key Stages, which begs a question about how the two sets of ratings are expected to relate to each other. Dearing used several paragraphs in this interim report to address this issue and his observations are worth quoting:

> Reference has been made to teacher assessment. It has often been argued during the Review that this is a more valid and more efficient way of gathering summative data on pupil and school performance. It can take place continuously through the year or at times which are well-fitted to stages of learning. In that sense, it is said to be more efficient because the tests disrupt normal teaching and consume scarce financial resources.

> But teacher assessment needs to be moderated if parents and teachers across the system, for example in receiving schools, can be confident about the standard being applied. The monitoring of national performance or of performance across a locality depends upon information related to a national standard. . . . Effective moderation is therefore necessary. Moderation, by peer groups of teachers or by external audit, with schools' procedures and the outcomes evaluated, perhaps through school inspections, has however, its own significant opportunity costs. It cannot readily produce the same consistency of standards as national tests. The statutory tests are, therefore, a valuable means of moderating teacher assessment. If well conceived and well conducted, they also provide reliable information related to a national standard.
> (Dearing, 1993, paras 5.13 and 5.14)

It appeared that what Dearing was proposing, at this time, was that the combination of 'group moderation by teachers' and 'moderation by external audit', which was effectively the basis of the models emerging in the LEAs and schools that we have studied, should be supplemented if not replaced by a form of moderation by 'reference test' on the grounds of cost and reliability. This was a cause of some concern because, for reasons outlined earlier, 'moderation by reference test' was the least favoured of TGAT's (1988a) original three options.

Interestingly, Dearing's final report made no further mention of this particular proposal and one might infer that the consultation on the interim report raised significant objections to this idea. Instead, the final report indicates a 'pulling back' from any firm recommendation pending the results of a number of projects commissioned by SCAA to develop systems of quality assurance in and across schools. It appeared that the work carried out in some LEAs over the past three years was being ignored.

All that Dearing was prepared to say at this point on the moderation of teacher assessment was that

> One of the possibilities currently being canvassed is that OFSTED and the Office of Her Majesty's Chief Inspector of Schools in Wales should contribute to the moderation of teacher assessment during their four-yearly inspections of schools (five-yearly in Wales). On the assumption that schools in a locality come together to form groups to moderate their assessments and that these groups are large enough for one school in the group to be inspected each year, this might enable each school in the group to benefit from regular external advice about standards of assessment.
>
> (Dearing, 1994, para. 9.2)

This possible approach appears to 'write out' the involvement of LEAs except in so far as LEA inspectors/advisers are also registered inspectors with the Office for Standards in Education (OFSTED). It also assumes that OFSTED inspectors will have access to 'national norms' by which to judge the standards of assessment observed in individual schools. Although OFSTED is to publish a new framework for inspection in April 1994, the current handbook gives no indication of national norms. The East Anglian AIAA group, which counts a number of OFSTED registered inspectors in its membership, regarded it as 'unprofessional and lacking in credibility to assume that this procedure was currently feasible'.

Of course, it is fair to point out that this suggestion was made with regard to the non-core subjects, and with KS3 particularly in mind.

Nevertheless, there appeared little enthusiasm in Dearing's final report for extending the present arrangements for audit moderation at KS1 in the core subjects.

> At present, audit-moderation takes place for the core subjects at Key Stage 1, covering both the standard tests and tasks and broader teacher assessment. . . . An extension of the arrangements to cover teacher assessment in the non-core foundation subjects would, however, require substantial extra resources. Careful evaluation of its benefits needs to be undertaken before it can be justified.
>
> (Dearing, 1994, para. 9.10)

On a more positive note, Dearing had clearly appreciated the value of a number of the developments outlined in earlier sections of this chapter and recognised the need for SCAA to continue to support moderation by teachers by the production of exemplar material (Dearing, 1994, para. 9.4) and the provision of 'high quality standard test and task material which can be used flexibly, and on a voluntary basis' (Dearing, 1994, para. 9.5). He also commended the growing practice of keeping 'a *small* number of samples of work for each child to demonstrate progress and attainment' (individual children's portfolios) as well as the development of school portfolios to assist the process of audit moderation (Dearing, 1994, Appendix 6).

Taken together, Dearing's two reports convey a somewhat confused picture of what moderation procedures might look like in the future. They appear to make reference to all three TGAT options: moderation by reference test, moderation by inspection and group moderation by teachers. What is clear, however, is that the emphasis has shifted away from quality assurance of assessment processes and towards quality control of assessment outcomes. As Dearing put it, 'The purpose of audit-moderation is to verify the accuracy of the assessment judgements made by the school and promote consistency between schools' (Dearing, 1994, Appendix 6, para. 25).

Quality control within quality assurance

Dearing was correct, of course, in his observation that current models of moderation, as exemplified in our research, are costly. They require the provision of extensive training of teachers, the appointment of hundreds of moderators and the development of materials, procedures and practices which have been unknown to most schools hitherto. However, they are only excessively costly if such elaborate systems serve *only* to produce accurate assessment results, that is to fulfil the quality control function. If this were the case then they would not have enjoyed the kind of support among teachers that our evidence indicates. The reason for advocating such models is not that they can turn teachers into good examiners but that it can help them become *better teachers*. Many teachers believed that they had developed professionally over the last three years and they they had acquired skills of observing and analysing children's learning and refining their judgements in relation to both assessment and curriculum. If the quality assurance systems described above are seen in these terms, then they are delivering much more than dependable assessment results and the costs can be attributed to a much wider range of educational purposes. Undoubtedly the achievement of these purposes needs to be improved but if the quality assurance system is an appropriate vehicle then it may well be worth the investment.

The question of whether a professional model of quality assurance can deliver dependable assessment results which will be credible to a sceptical public is, in some ways, more difficult to answer. It is possible to argue that reliable outcomes will flow *ipso facto* from the putting in place of sound assessment processes and procedures. Thus quality assurance focusing on assessment processes and tasks should *guarantee* the quality of assessment results. On the other hand, there is little hard evidence that this idealised view has ever been fully realised in practice. What may be preferable, therefore, is the conceptualisation of a quality assurance system that, instead of being distinguished from quality control, actually incorporates it. This could be a way of confronting the problem of professional quality assurance systems being necessary but not sufficient to engender confidence in the quality of assessment outcomes.

There is a sense in which the East Anglian LEAs were already going along this road by the provision and encouragement of agreement trials at intra-school and inter-school level, by the provision of sample materials to indicate common standards and by strengthening the audit role of local moderators. If this 'quality control within quality assurance' could be made more robust – and its costs justified in terms of educational improvement and professional development – then it might just be possible to argue against the introduction of predominantly 'external' quality control systems whether in the form of OFSTED inspections or the development of reference tests for scaling purposes. Unfortunately the latter will have an appeal, on grounds of simplicity and cost, to many of those outside of education. Not only will these arguments have to be confronted, but politicians, particularly, will need to be made aware that the question of the competence of OFSTED inspectors to judge school assessments in relation to national standards will need to be addressed.

Similarly, they should be disabused of any idea that the creation of simple 'rigorous' tests that are valid and reliable in the context of the National Curriculum is an easy task. The experience of the past three years suggests that this is not so.

Acknowledgements

I am grateful to Colin Conner with whom I worked in equal partnership on the research reported in this chapter. I also owe a great debt to the six LEAs that sponsored the research and to all the advisers and teachers who supplied the data. However, interpretations and opinions expressed in this chapter do not necessarily represent the views of the LEAs and any errors or omissions are mine alone.

References

Angoff, W. H. (1974) Criterion-referencing, norm-referencing and the SAT, *College Board Review*, Vol. 92, pp. 2–5.

Black, P., Harlen, W. and Orgee, A. (1984) *Standards of Performance: Expectations and Reality*, APU occasional paper, DES, London.

Conner, C. and James, M. (1991) *Bedfordshire Assessment Training, 1991: An Independent Evaluation*, Cambridge Institute of Education.

Conner, C. and James, M. (1993) *Assuring Quality in Assessments in Schools in Six LEAs, 1993*, Cambridge Institute of Education.

DES/WO (1988a) *Task Group on Assessment and Testing: A Report*, DES/WO, London.

Daugherty, R. (1994) *National Curriculum Assessment: A Review of Policy 1988–93*, Falmer Press, London.

Dearing, Sir R. (1993a) Personal communication, 29 July.

Dearing, Sir R. (1993b) *The National Curriculum and its Assessment: Interim Report*, NCC and SEAC, London and York.

Dearing, Sir R. (1994) *The National Curriculum and its Assessment: Final Report*, SCAA, London.

HMI (Her Majesty's Inspectorate) (1994) *Assessment, Recording and Reporting: Key Stages 1, 2 and 3: Fourth Year 1992–93*, OFSTED, London.

James, M. and Conner, C. (1992) *Moderation at Key Stage One across Four LEAs, 1992*, University of Cambridge Institute of Education.

James, M. and Conner, C. (1993) Are reliability and validity achievable in National Curriculum assessment? Some observations on moderation at Key Stage 1 in 1992, *The Curriculum Journal*, Vol. 4, no. 1, pp. 5–19.

SEAC (Schools Examination and Assessment Council) (1991) *National Curriculum Assessment. Assessment Arrangements for Core and other Foundation Subjects. A Moderator's Handbook 1991/2*, SEAC, London.

Wiliam, D. (1993) Validity, dependability and reliability in National Curriculum assessment, *The Curriculum Journal*, Vol. 4, no. 3 (Autumn), pp. 335–50.

8

TOWARDS QUALITY IN ASSESSMENT

Wynne Harlen

Assessment is an inexact matter and can never be an exact one. There are many reasons for this, the most obvious being that we cannot ever know what is inside the head of a person and we must judge learning from what the person can do in particular circumstances. This means that we do not know what they can do in other circumstances; the generalisability of assessments is limited. A second reason is that, in education, we are often trying to describe something – a pupil's skill or knowledge – that is changing. Whatever the source of information, whether tests or teachers' assessment, the result is 'where the pupil seems to be' in development rather than anything more definite. This is not a failure of assessment; it is only common sense, for if pupils are learning and developing, they will be constantly changing and it will not be possible to pin-point where they are in their development with any precision.

A third set of reasons for inexactness – a term I prefer to 'error', which suggests that a 'correct' assessment exists if only we were able to overcome all the obstacles in our way – has been the concern of this book. These are the circumstances outside the pupil which can affect the result of assessment. Although we cannot aspire to exactness, there is every reason for not adding to inexactness which would make assessment in some circumstances, for example where it is used for selection, unfair, and in other circumstances, where it is used for decisions about teaching, useless.

Copyright © 1994, Wynne Harlen

From the discussion and evidence presented in this book the main reasons, external to the pupil, for variation in assessment can be summarised as follows:

Differences in interpretation by teachers or assessors of what is being assessed

These differences are the inevitable consequence of having to communicate, in brief statements, often complex messages about skills and understandings to be learned and assessed. Such problems were reported in Chapter 5 by Black as being encountered in the context of specifying performance criteria in National Certificate modules. He added, however, that they were relatively easily overcome 'particularly by strategies which encourage staff to share their understandings and their difficulties'.

Differences in the tasks, or contexts surrounding tasks, when assessment takes place, including how much help is given

This may seem to be more a problem for teacher assessment than for external assessment, since one of its main justifications is that it allows teachers to set tasks which may vary from one individual to another to suit interests and circumstances. Daugherty points out in Chapter 5 that, when assessment is for certification, 'unless the moderation procedure impacts in some way on the type of task set and on the circumstances under which candidates complete the task, a major source of unreliability will remain'. However, it is also the case that identical tasks and conditions do not imply identical opportunity, for pupils' motivation to respond differs in relation to the same task. This is not only important for younger pupils; Satterly makes the point in Chapter 3 that setting uninteresting topics or tasks can be a problem in external examinations. Not only do such tasks fail to give students opportunity to show what they can do, but they may also fail adequately to represent the domain being tested.

Differences in the specificity of criteria or mark scheme to be applied in making a judgement

This is a further aspect of the difficulty of communicating intentions and criteria effectively. Daugherty reports that examining boards receive many requests for help from teachers in interpreting guidelines for setting tasks and for using marking schemes. A similar dilemma exists here as in National Curriculum assessment; the more specific the criteria, the more statements there have to be to cover possible responses and the more chance of excluding unusual but acceptable responses; but the more general the criteria the more chance of the interpretations of individual staff differing and of responses being accepted which were not intended to be acceptable. The extent to which teachers or markers are expected to go outside the strict limits will vary according to the degree of specificity of the criteria and is not always obvious.

Taking other circumstances into account in assessment as well as the overt response to a task and the intended criteria

In Chapter 5 Black reports that in an early stage of the introduction of the new modular structure in Scottish further education, a higher level of performance was expected by some lecturers of mature adult students than of younger school-leavers. Similarly studies at Key Stage 1 found teachers making allowances for some children and at times using knowledge of performance in other contexts to make judgements which should have been made only on information from the standard task.

How the judgements are translated into grades, marks, comments or action

Research reported by Satterly indicates that in the context of external examinations the greatest source of unreliability in assigning grades occurs at the boundaries between one grade and the next. The more highly differentiated the grades the greater the possibility of misallocation. In the context of the National Curriculum assessment, marks are not translated into levels, rather judgements are made directly about the extent to which criteria at one level or the next are met. There are differences as to whether this should be a holistic judgement based, for example, on what the criteria for Level 3 mean in terms of 'Level-3-ness' or whether there should be an atomistic application of multiple specific criteria followed by the use of some formula to say whether Level 3 has been achieved (as mentioned by James in Chapter 7). Experience in GCSE and in the National Curriculum suggests that teachers begin with a mechanical atomistic approach and use a more holistic one as they become more familiar with the criteria and confident in their judgements.

Differences between subjects in the meaning of levels or grades

Comparability in assessment among different academic subjects is often implied by using similar grade labels, although the basis of equality is rarely based in any sound epistemology. In Chapter 2 Broadfoot reports the practice in Australia of putting results for all subjects on a common scale as part of the procedure for determining entrance to tertiary education. In the GCSE, although there is no scaling, the same grade labels are used. There is little similarity between a B in French and a B in geography except that both match the very different B grade descriptors. In the National Curriculum assessment, the basis for equality of levels across subjects relied on the element of norm-referencing used in specifying criteria, to which reference is made by James in Chapter 7. Thus in locating Level 4 as that which is attained by the majority of eleven-year-olds, criteria were set up which reflected this norm for all subjects.

There is a sequence in this list in terms of what happens in making an assessment, the earlier items relating to planning and then carrying out the process and the later to its product. However, all are involved to some degree in any assessment, whether formal or informal and whether by teachers or by examination boards. Various procedures for moderation, many of which have been described in earlier chapters, have been designed to reduce the effect of one or more of these sources of variation. However, there have been reminders in all the chapters of this book, but particularly in Chapters 2, 5 and 7, that decisions as to which procedure(s) to use are not always influenced by the single aim of achieving high reliability and validity. Tradition, the status of the assessment, its role, and above all the political context, have weight which often outbalances technical or educational arguments. The result is that what is regarded as providing credible assessment results in one educational system is not necessarily seen to do so in another. This does not of course, diminish the value of examining the evidence about reliability and validity, for the price of taking a particular decision has to be known. Thus the decision to reduce the extent of teacher-assessed work in GCSE has to be seen in terms of a decrease in validity and in teacher commitment.

Which approach to moderation?

Our focus has been on assessment carried out by teachers and the steps which can be taken to make this more dependable, but we have also considered the dependability of external assessments and the steps taken to improve that so that both teacher and external assessment can be judged in the same way. Often more stringent demands are made of innovations than are expected of what they replace, and it would seem from the discussion in Chapters 3 and 6 that educational assessment is no exception.

Nevertheless it is important to increase public confidence in assessment by teachers even though the greater confidence in external assessment may be misplaced. As the list of sources of inexactness above indicates, moderation must be concerned with all parts of the process of assessment and with what is in the teacher's mind as well as with public procedures. Thus we have argued that improvement in teacher assessment is intimately related to professional development and that therefore this should be a major factor in deciding how to go about moderation. However, as Gipps and James point out in their commentaries on experience of moderation of teacher assessment at Key Stage 1 (Chapters 4 and 7) professional development is time consuming and costly and these aspects cannot be ignored. But statistical and bureaucratic procedures also have their cost and thus should also be judged in these terms. More generally, we can draw out from the discussion of moderation procedures in earlier chapters a number of aspects which should be considered in comparing their advantages and disadvantages. Table 8.1 does this in terms of six aspects: the extent to which the moderation procedures are bureaucratically controlled, their contribution to professional development of teachers, their demands in terms of time and costs and their impact on the process and the product of assessment. Judgements, which must be regarded as rough guidelines only, are indicated by a rating from one to three. The justification for these ratings derives from the evidence of procedures presented throughout this book.

Looking across the rows of Table 8.1 gives a set of profiles of moderation procedures. In each one, not surprisingly, costs and time tend to be

Table 8.1 Profiles of moderation procedures

Procedure	Bureau-cratic	Contribu-ion to professional development	Time	Cost	Impact on process	Impact on product
Statistical – reference tests	•••	–	•	•	–	•••
Inspection of samples	•	•	•	•	–	••
External examining	•	•	••	•••	•	••
Group moderation of grades	•	••	••	•••	••	••
Defining criteria	–	••	••	•	•	••
Exemplification	–	••	•	•	••	••
Centre approval	–	••	•	•	••	••
Moderator visits	–	••	•••	•••	•••	•
Group moderation	–	•••	•••	•••	•••	••

similar. It is also relatively easy to pick out those we have described as quality control since these have a high impact on the product of assessment and small impact on the process. However, those described as quality assurance have an impact on both process and product, supporting the claim by Gipps at the end of Chapter 4 that a focus on quality assurance – improving the quality of the process – will inevitably also lead to an improved quality of product and hence greater consistency in standards and confidence in assessment results.

Looking within columns provides a means of comparing approaches in terms of specific characteristics, although the interdependence of the characteristics must not be forgotten. As might be expected, this shows that procedures involving the movement of people are expensive. However, both this and the time aspects are also dependent on the scale of the operation. For example, external examining in higher education may be acceptable in terms of time and cost, but visits of moderators to all schools for National Curriculum assessment would not be because of the much greater number of schools than of higher education institutions.

As with assessment procedures, so with moderation approaches: their acceptability will depend upon tradition and social values as much as on rational arguments. The differences, and the choice of one or another can be described but not explained. Thus the statement about quality of moderation which we offered in Chapter 1 (as being *the process which optimises the reliability of an assessment at a cost which is balanced by the benefits in terms of the purposes of the assessment and contribution to professional development*) is one which finds favour in the UK, where teachers generally value participation in decision-making and seek to use professional judgement in making assessments. This preference is reinforced by embracing objectives of education which extend far beyond the type of knowledge and skills development which can be assessed by formal written tests. Thus, if the professional development element is seen as a *sine qua non*, then Table 8.1 suggests that group moderation would be judged as being of the highest quality, all other things being equal. However, the other aspects, particularly the practical aspects of time and cost, cannot be ignored.

The alternatives which have lower cost but fairly high impact on process and product and on professional development appear to be 'exemplification' and 'centre approval'. The value of exemplification has been noted in several studies (for example, in Chapters 4 and 7), whilst centre approval is seen as the appropriate course in further education in Scotland. Making schools into 'approved centres' of assessment will require them to have in place procedures for ensuring quality assurance and control and the appointment of assessment co-ordinators has already taken place in some primary as well as secondary schools. The increase in professional responsibility for quality in assessment is to be welcomed. However, in the context of schools being increasingly placed in competition with one another, there is a danger that it will be seen necessary for public confidence to provide some measure of external control to ensure consistency of standards across schools. Unfortunately the means of doing this through school inspectors or visiting peer groups is not seen to be as effective as using statutory tests, according to the Dearing Review; it seems that a return to bureaucratic control of teacher assessment through national tests is the SCAA's preferred model. The same difficulties have, of course, arisen in relation to further education in Scotland but, as Black notes in Chapter 5, there the introduction of an element of external assessment would be seen as a retrograde step; the route of enhancing quality though professional development is preferred even in the context of certification. The contrary decision taken at the school level seems to have been made on the basis of a different view of the professional responsibility of teachers.

In our view, based on evidence presented here, it is possible to enhance the quality of teachers' assessments through moderation procedures which support professional development. By doing so we would achieve assessment results which would give dependable information about pupils' and students' performance across the wide range of aims of education. To do otherwise sets up a self-fulfilling prophecy which lowers teachers' professional status and so reduces public confidence in their judgements.

INDEX